ANKOKU BUTŌ

ANKOKU BUTŌ

The Premodern and Postmodern Influences on the Dance of Utter Darkness

Susan Blakeley Klein

East Asia Program
Cornell University
Ithaca, New York 14853

The Cornell East Asia Series is published by the Cornell University East Asia Program (distinct from Cornell University Press). We publish affordably priced books on a variety of scholarly topics relating to East Asia as a service to the academic community and the general public. Standing orders, which provide for automatic billing and shipping of each title in the series upon publication, are accepted.

If after review by internal and external readers a manuscript is accepted for publication, it is published on the basis of camera-ready copy provided by the volume author. Each author is thus responsible for any necessary copy-editing and for manuscript formatting. Address submission inquiries to CEAS Editorial Board, East Asia Program, Cornell University, Ithaca, New York 14853-7601.

Number 49 in the Cornell East Asia Series
Copyright © 1988 by Susan Blakeley Klein. All rights reserved
ISSN 1050-2955
ISBN 0-939657-49-X pb
Printed in the United States of America
18 17 16 15 14 13 12 11 10 09 08 07 06 03   9 8 7 6 5 4 3

Cover photo: Ohno Kazuo performing "Admiring La Argentina," courtesy of Ohno Kazuo; © Tsukamoto Hiro. Cover design by Karen K. Smith.

⊗ The paper in this book meets the requirements for permanence of ISO 9706:1994.

Dedication

For Stuart

Table of Contents

Acknowledgments

This essay began as an M.A. thesis four years ago, and so by now the number of people to whom I am indebted for support and guidance is far too great to be contained in just one page. In Japan, I would first and foremost like to thank Ohno Kazuo, whose teaching (both formally through classes and informally through personal conversations) was a wonderful source of inspiration and encouragement. I'd also like to thank Ohno Yoshito and the Ohno family as a whole for their many kindnesses to me during my stay in Japan (1987-1989); I have many fond memories of our times together. Mizohata Toshio helped me in countless ways and offered excellent suggestions on a late draft of the manuscript. On several occasions dance critic Gōda Nario took time from a busy schedule to discuss the Butō aesthetic in depth; I also benefited from informal conversations with Ichikawa Miyabi and Nakamura Fumiaki. Finally, I'd like to thank Nakajima Natsu for her supportive and intellectually stimulating friendship.

In the United States, those whom I would particularly like to thank include: Fumiko Dobashi, for her friendship, as well as for her patient and painstaking work with me on the translations; Prof. Sally Banes, Mellon Fellow at Cornell for 1985-1986, whose course on postmodern dance provided me with a cross-cultural context for my study of Butō, and whose inspired editing moved the first two drafts of this thesis far along the road to its final form; Prof. Victor Koschmann for his suggestions on ways to revise and amplify the original thesis, especially with regard to the political and intellectual context of the 1960's; Prof. Karen Brazell, whose courses in traditional Japanese performing arts laid the groundwork for this thesis, whose comments on the various drafts were invaluable, and whose firm good sense kept me from wandering off into the kind of "never-never land" of speculation that Butō all too easily tempts one into. I'd also like to thank Roger Jagoda; without his help on the myriad computer problems that came up, this thesis would never have seen the light of day. Finally, I would like to thank my thesis advisor, Prof. Brett de Bary, for encouraging me to do research on a subject about which neither she nor I had any prior knowledge. Her confidence in me was a major source of support, as was her careful reading and rereading of the various drafts and translations. I simply could not have done it without her help.

Nakajima Natsu in "Nanakusa" section from <u>Niwa</u> (The Garden). Photographed by Nourit Masson-Sekine.

INTRODUCTION

"Modern dance is too talkative and expresses too much"
Ohno Kazuo

"Creating unerasable impressions is our business"
Amagatsu Ushio

On May 24, 1959, as intellectuals and artists all across Japan were gearing up for protest against the U.S.-Japan Mutual Defense Treaty, Hijikata Tatsumi held his first major performance: Kinjiki (Forbidden Colors),[1] based on the novel by Mishima Yukio. Danced by two males, a young boy and an older man, the climax of the work came when a live chicken was strangled to death over the boy's prone body. With this performance, "Ankoku Butō" (the Dance of Utter Darkness) made its first appearance and simultaneously managed to scoop the punk rock movement by a good twenty years.

The Butō movement was the product of an attempt by Hijikata Tatsumi and Ohno Kazuo (who although not directly involved with the production of Forbidden Colors itself, played an essential role in the formation of the Butō aesthetic) to create a specifically Japanese dance form that would transcend the constraints of both Western modern dance and traditional Japanese dance. It was a provocative form of social criticism, a response to the Japanese avant garde's disenchantment with Western cultural and political dominance, and it had an enormous

---

[1]Where possible, titles of dances are given in the original Japanese followed by my translation in English (occasionally, however, I have only an English title for the work). Thereafter I will refer to the work by a shortened form of the title, usually taken from the English. Japanese names are given in the traditional Japanese style, family name first, given name second.

1

influence on young artists and intellectuals of the early 1960's, particularly in theater.

The word ankoku literally means "pitch black"; butō is made up of the character "bu" [舞], which means "to dance" (the same "bu" that is found in Kabuki [歌舞伎]), and the character "to" [踏], which means "to step or tread." The ending "ha" [派][2] means group or party (as in "political party"). Some critics have seen the butō of Ankoku Butō as evoking "reverberations of ancient ritual dances,"[3] but in fact, before Ankoku Butō was invented, the word butō's most general use was as a catch-all term for any dance that did not fall into the category of traditional Japanese dance (generically referred to as buyō). Therefore, the waltz, flamenco, and even belly dancing would all be categorized as butō in Japanese. It is only in the last ten years, with the emergence of a second and then third generation of choreographers influenced by the original Ankoku Butō-ha, but who have aims and principles that differ from the founders' ideas, that the "Ankoku" has, for the most part, been dropped, and that "Butō" has come to signify the entire spectrum of dance that has, in one way or another, been influenced by Ohno Kazuo and Hijikata Tatsumi.[4]

This essay is not intended as a definitive explanation of the Butō movement. Rather, it should be looked upon as an introduction, for the general reader interested in dance and performance as well as for the Japanalogist, to the history of Butō and to some of its goals and techniques. Not only do the large number of people influenced by the movement and the

---

[2]The "ha" of Ankoku Butō-ha, can be taken in two senses: one sense is that of a group with similar principles and goals (an equivalent in English might be an artistic circle surrounding a charismatic leader, for example the Bloomsbury group); the second and overlapping meaning is that of a "movement" (for example, the Surrealist movement). This ambiguity leads to a certain amount of confusion about exactly what the term "Ankoku Butō-ha" refers to: although the original members of Ankoku Butō-ha (the group) disbanded in 1966, dance influenced by Hijikata continued to be called Ankoku Butō-ha (the movement). It was only in the 1970's that the movement's name was shortened to Butō.

[3]Oyama Shigeō, "Amagatsu Ushio: Avant-garde Choreographer," Japan Quarterly 32 (January-March 1985), pp. 69-70.

[4]In order to try to differentiate between the two meanings of butō, here and in the translations in the appendix, I have used "Butō" to mean the dance movement, and translated the other butō as "western-style dance."

wide range of styles that have evolved from it conspire against coming up with a single all-inclusive definition; but the philosophy of Butō itself is vehemently opposed to any critical interpretation that might limit the possible meanings evoked in the viewer. Therefore, I have tried to tread lightly here and to indicate clearly when the comments and ideas come from the artists themselves and where my own speculation comes into play.

When I set out to do research on Butō in 1985 I was surprised at the paucity of materials in English that were available--at that time virtually nothing but short reviews by American and European critics. When faced with the sudden emergence of the Butō phenomenon on the Western dance scene, these critics, having no knowledge of the artistic (not to mention social and political) context out of which Butō developed in Japan, could only interpret what they saw in terms of the development of American and European modern dance, and so were of only limited help. And unfortunately, in 1985-86 when much of my research was done, there were not even any collections of essays on Butō in Japanese--writing on Butō was still scattered among a number of theater and dance journals that were not easily available in the United States. For the history of the Butō movement I depended instead on personal interviews with Butō artists and on articles in Japanese that those artists gave me. Since Hijikata's death in January 1986 this situation has been remedied somewhat, mostly through the the efforts of the Japanese critics Gōda Nario and Kuniyoshi Kazuko in cooperation with Hijikata's widow, Motofuji Akiko. I was therefore able to use a chronology of Hijikata's life prepared by Gōda and Kuniyoshi, as well as several personal conversations with Gōda in April 1988 to confirm the facts presented here.

The essay is divided into three sections: the first outlines the history and origin of the movement; the second examines some of the philosophy and presents a selection of the many techniques that are shared generally by Butō choreographers; the third attempts to show how some of those techniques are used concretely by analyzing a specific dance, Niwa (The Garden), which was performed by the Butō group Muteki-sha at The Asia Society in New York City on September 27 and 28, 1985.

Nakajima Natsu and Maezawa Yuriko in "The Dream" section from <u>Niwa</u> (The Garden). Photographed by Nourit Masson-Sekine.

Chapter One

THE ORIGIN AND HISTORICAL CONTEXT OF ANKOKU BUTŌ

The Butō dance movement originated mainly through the creative interaction of two powerful and charismatic dancers: Ohno Kazuo and Hijikata Tatsumi (Ohno's son, Ohno Yoshito, who studied with Hijikata and played the part of the young man in Forbidden Colors is said to have had considerable influence as well[1]). Both Ohno and Hijikata were born and grew up in Northern Japan (Tohoku): Ohno was born in the fishing village of Hakodate in 1906, Hijikata was born Yoneyama Kunio in a farming village in Akita prefecture in 1928. For Hijikata in particular the fact that he was born in the Northern "provincial" part of Japan came to have a great deal of significance, as he believed that the places in which we grow up, as well as those who surround us, impress themselves upon our bodies in an unconscious, but nevertheless powerful way.[2] Both knew great poverty: Ohno recalls that when he was in junior high school his youngest sibling died in his arms because they didn't have enough money to take the child to the doctor.[3] Hijikata remembered vividly the day that his older sister was sold into prostitution (a common practice in the economically depressed farming

---

[1]In reference to his son's influence on his work, Ohno has said, "if my son were not around, perhaps I wouldn't have been able to dance--there is always a conflict between the two of us when I create a piece, and only through that conflict can I finish the piece." Ohno Kazuo, "The Origins of Ankoku Butō," audiotape of lecture delivered at Cornell University, 25 November 1985. Hereafter cited as: Ohno, Cornell lecture.

[2]This idea of the body as a repository for memory had its fullest expression in Hijikata's 1972 work, Tōhoku Kabuki, in which Hijikata used the gestures and movements of Tōhoku people of the early Showa era (i.e., the period of Hijikata's childhood) as a basis for the dance.

[3]Ohno, Cornell lecture.

villages of the time). In Hijikata's autobiographical work <u>Yameru Mai Hime</u> (A Dancer's Sickness) he writes: "One day, a casual glance around the house revealed that the furniture was all gone. Furniture and household utensils are something you can't help but notice. And around that time my older sister, who always sat on the veranda, suddenly disappeared. I thought to myself, maybe this is just something older sisters naturally do--disappear from the house."[4]

Hijikata was the youngest of 11 children and he adored this older sister who had raised him; dance critic Gōda Nario has pinpointed the devastating experience of her loss as the motivating force behind Hijikata's dance, noting that Hijikata began letting his hair grow long in the 1960's in the belief that this act would help his sister to live on within him.[5] Ohno, on the other hand, was the oldest of thirteen, and a number of his dances have dealt with his relationship to his mother, particularly his feelings of guilt for what he calls his "selfishness" (<u>katte na koto</u>) towards her.[6]

Although the two dancers came from similar backgrounds, however, their temperaments were quite different: Ohno himself has said that the creative energy that produced Ankoku Butō was the outcome of the collaboration of two men with personalities on the extreme ends of the spectrum; Ohno sees himself as the light, Hijikata as the dark, both poles of which were necessary to create the energy that is Butō.[7]

One of Japan's truly great solo dancers, Ohno's style was formed in the 20's and 30's, the period when German modern dance was just beginning to be introduced to Japan. An excellent athlete in highschool, his first exposure to German dance was through the Rudolph Bode Expression Exercises that he studied in Tokyo at Japan Athletic School (later called Japan Athletic College). After graduating he began teaching physical education at Kanto Gakuin High School (a private Christian school in Yokohama), and sometime during the first five years he taught there he was baptized as a Protestant

---

[4]Hijikata Tatsumi, <u>Yameru Mai Hime</u> (A Dancer's Sickness), (Tokyo: Hakusuisha, 1983), pp. 89-90.

[5]Gōda Nario, "Ankoku Butō ni Tsuite" (On Ankoku Butō), <u>Butō: Nikutai no Suriarisutotachi</u> (Butō: Surrealists of the Flesh), ed. Hanaga Mitsutoshi (Tokyo: Gendai Shokan, 1983), unpaginated. Page numbers cited hereafter refer to translation in appendix. For this citation, see p. 84.

[6]Dances of the last ten years with this theme include <u>Okâsan</u> (Mother), <u>Ozen: Dream of a Fetus</u>, and <u>The Dead Sea</u>.

[7]Ohno, interview with author, 25 November 1985.

Christian on the beach at Kamakura. Ohno continued a full time career teaching physical education concomitant with his career in dance, until his retirement in 1980. He says he was first inspired to dance in 1929 when he sat with a friend in the top balcony of the Imperial Theater in Tokyo watching La Argentina (Antonia Mercé), the famous flamenco dancer: "From the first moment, I was moved almost beyond bearing. I was totally stunned. This was the encounter that changed my life."[8]

Seeing Harald Kreutzberg dance in 1934 influenced him to study for one year with Ishii Baku[9] (who had toured Europe in the 1920's and seen Mary Wigman dance), and then with Eguchi Takaya, who had brought back "neuer Tanz" from his study at Mary Wigman's institute in Germany. In a personal interview Ohno remarked that Kreutzberg's influence was different than La Argentina's in that when he watched Kreutzberg dance he was struck by his sublime technique, but when he watched La Argentina dance, her effect on him was such that technique was no longer a consideration. This latter effect is what Ohno has said he especially wanted to recreate in one of his most famous works, Admiring La Argentina, but in fact, this stress on personal charisma over "mere" technical virtuosity underlies all his work.[10]

Ohno's career was interrupted, and his style virtually frozen in time, by World War II, so that his first public recital did not come until he was forty-three (1949) when he danced with Andō Mitsuko (another disciple of Eguchi Takaya) at Kanda Public Hall in Tokyo.[11] It's unclear when and where Ohno and Hijikata first met, but according to Lizzie Slater, a long time Butō aficionado and sometime manager of the Butō groups Sankai Juku and Muteki-sha, it was Ohno's early performances with Andō that brought him into contact with Hijikata Tatsumi. Ohno Yoshito, who was still in highschool

---

[8]Ohno Kazuo, "Encounter with Argentina," trans. Maehata Noriko, Stone Lion Review, no. 9 (Spring 1982), p. 45.

[9]Western style dance was introduced to Japan by Giovanni V. Rossi who was hired by the Imperial Theater in Tokyo in 1912 to teach European operatic theater and creative ballet. Ishii Baku, who was Rossi's most talented dance pupil, was the first Japanese to perform a Western-style dance in public: in June of 1916 he performed a "dance poem" inspired by the work of W.B. Yeats.

[10]Ohno, interview with author, 1 July 1986.

[11]The pieces included: Ennui for the City with Andō Mitsuko and three solo pieces, Devil Cry, Tango, and First Flower of a Linden Tree.

at the time, remembers Hijikata coming to their home in Yokohama around 1954.[12]

Hijikata had studied dance for a short while with Masumura Katsuko, a student of Eguchi Takaya, in Akita City. He came to Tokyo for the first time in 1949; during this initial visit he happened to see Andō and Ohno dance at Kanda Public Hall and was quite struck by Ohno's dance. Caught up in the Western-style dance "craze" that was sweeping Japan at the time, he moved permanently to Tokyo in 1952, and began studying with Eguchi Takaya and Andō Mitsuko.[13] In 1953 Hijikata performed a piece choreographed by Andō on television, and it was around this time that he finally met Ohno. Ohno offered Hijikata his own unique interpretation of German dance methods; Hijikata brought to the collaboration his interest in using the works of such "decadent" literary and artistic figures as Genet, Lautréamont, Marquis de Sade, and Aubrey Beardsley. At the time of his first stage appearance in 1954 he changed his name to Hijikata Kunio, and became a member of Andō's group, "Unique Ballet." He continued to participate in Unique Ballet's yearly performances until the late 1950's when he changed his name to Hijikata Tatsumi and founded his own group, "Hijikata Tatsumi Dance Experience." In November of 1961, he gave a name to the dance movement he had created, retroactively christening it "Ankoku Butō-ha."[14]

As mentioned previously, the first performance of Ankoku Butō came in 1959, and in Forbidden Colors many of the qualities that have since come

---

[12]Lizzie Slater, "The Dead Begin to Run: Kazuo Ohno and Butoh Dance." Dance Theatre Journal, London (Winter 1986), pp. 7-8.

[13]When the postwar occupation lifted the wartime censorship on Western dance and drama, first Tokyo and then all of Japan was swept by what could only be called a "craze" for Western-style dance. Although in the beginning ballet eclipsed modern dance in popularity, the number of modern dance schools and studios increased steadily throughout the 1950's, supported and periodically revitalized by visits from the major modern dance companies of the period. For a detailed discussion of the economic ramifications of postwar cultural developments in Japan, see Thomas R.H. Havens, Artist and Patron in Postwar Japan (Princeton: Princeton University Press, 1982). According to Havens, the visit of Martha Graham's dance company in 1955 had a particularly strong effect on the shape that mainstream dance took in the 50's and 60's in Japan, and it was often towards Graham-influenced work that Butō directed its anti-Western antagonism.

[14]In the 1 July 1986 interview, Ohno identified three members of Ankoku Butō-ha: Ohno Yoshito, Ishii Mitsutaka and Kasai Akira.

to epitomize the Butō movement were already in evidence. Hijikata eliminated a number of the supports upon which mainstream dance leaned at that time: music (the dance was performed in complete silence), all interpretive program notes, and any dance techniques which went beyond what he felt were the realistic limits of the "natural" body.[15] By returning the focus of dance to the simplicity of a body that was in tune with nature, those involved with Ankoku Butō hoped to tap into the expressive energy and sense of life that they felt had been lost in contemporary society. The act of killing a chicken, with its primitive sacrificial overtones, was meant as an expression of the turbulent sexual passion which modern man suppresses but which still remains as a core of darkness at the heart of our existence. In the conclusion of Forbidden Colors this core of darkness expanded to cloak the entire stage: all that was left was the sound of the boy's footsteps escaping and the man pursuing him. It was from this conclusion--the performers were literally "dancing in the dark"--that Ankoku Butō-ha took its name.

Evoking images that were often grotesquely beautiful, and revelling in the shady, shameful underside of human behavior, the movement which Ankoku Butō spawned was very much a product of the bleak postwar landscape of Japan in the 1950's. It was a period of growing antagonism on the part of Japanese artists and intellectuals towards the superpowers (both the USA and the USSR), whom they held directly responsible for the threat of imminent destruction by nuclear war; America and Europe were also held responsible for the technology, closely bound up with Western modes of production, that was wreaking havoc on Japan's much idealized natural environment, thereby disrupting the traditional "sacred" bond between the Japanese and nature as well as contributing to a widespread sense of alienation, dehumanization, and loss of self-identity. This amorphous sense of disenchantment was given a concrete focus in 1959-1960 when the U.S.-Japan Mutual Defense Treaty (Nichibei Anzen Hoshō Jōyaku, or AMPO for short)[16] came up for a ten year renewal. The widespread debate and demonstrations that the controversial treaty occasioned acted as a catalyst for change in a number of areas, and Ankoku Butō was one of the first of the new artistic forms that emerged to challenge Western culture's hegemony.

---

[15]For this description of the performance of Forbidden Colors I am indebted to Gōda, "On Ankoku Butō," pp. 127-8.

[16]For an historical discussion of the 1960 Security Treaty Crisis, see George R. Packard, Protest in Tokyo: The Security Treaty Crisis of 1960 (Princeton: Princeton University Press, 1966).

However, in order to understand the particular form Ankoku Butō took, we will need to look more closely at the historical context out of which it arose. As a unique three-part fusion of elements from Western dance, Western theater, and traditional Japanese dance-theater, it was influenced by the 20th century history of all three forms in Japan.

The Historical Context of Western Theater
and Dance in Japan

The avant garde's reaction against Western cultural and political dominance has a number of interrelated components, not the least of which was that in both dance and theater of the 1950's, Western-influenced work had become the "establishment" and thus was ripe for overthrow by the younger generation. In regard to Western-style Japanese theater (called Shingeki, which literally means "new theater"), this feeling has been succinctly summed up by the critic Tsuno Kaitarō:

> Shingeki has become historical, it has become a tradition in its own right. The problem of the younger generation has been to come to terms with this tradition. For us modern European drama is no longer some Golden Ideal as yet out of reach. It is instead a pernicious, limiting influence...Shingeki no longer maintains the dialectical power to negate and transcend; rather, it has become an institution that itself demands to be transcended.[17]

The Shingeki movement was born in the early 20th century mainly through the efforts of Osanai Kaoru and Hijikata Yoshi,[18] as a radical attempt to establish a Japanese theater which would be patterned after the realistic theatrical style of Ibsen and Stanislavsky. It rejected both Kabuki and Shimpa, the theatrical form that in the late 19th century had attempted to achieve a synthesis of Western and native Japanese theater. In the 20's and 30's the

---

[17]Tsuno Kaitarō, "The Tradition of Modern Theatre in Japan," trans. David Goodman, Canadian Theater Review, no. 20 (Fall 1978), p. 11.

[18]Osanai Kaoru and Hijikata Yoshi (no relation to Hijikata Tatsumi) founded the Tsukiji Little Theater (Tsukiji Shōgekijō) in 1924 and in the four years that it lasted (until the death of Osanai in 1928) it trained most of the major actors and directors of the next 20-30 years. For an succinct discussion of the history of Shingeki and its pertinence to contemporary theater, see David Goodman, "New Japanese Theater," The Drama Review 15 (Spring 1971), pp. 154-168.

Shingeki movement became highly politicized through its association with the Japanese Communist Party (JCP), one result of which was Shingeki's strong commitment to Soviet socialist realism. These leftist leanings caused it to be heavily censored and repressed by the military government during World War II. The movement came back strong under the occupation, however, crystallizing into an orthodoxy that by the end of the 1950's had achieved a near monopoly on theater. Although Shingeki was dominated by directors and playwrights who had been trained in the socialist realism style of the 20's and 30's, many younger artists felt Shingeki's socialist realism was quickly becoming little different from mainstream Western-style realistic theater, and was no longer appropriate to the concerns of postwar Japan. However, because Shingeki was at least nominally political, and because many of its members were highly respected for the pacifist position they had taken in opposition to the war, it wasn't until the 1960 Security Treaty Crisis that the younger generation's differences with the older generation came to a head. The tension between young and old was intensified by the fact that many of the younger artists were also members of Zengakuren (the Japanese student movement).[19] Zengakuren had already broken with the JCP in 1958 when an anti-JCP faction, the Kyōsanshugisha Dōmei (the Communist League, or Bund) managed to take control of the Zengakuren leadership. Thus the rift that already existed between the JCP and Zengakuren paralleled and encouraged the rift that was just beginning to appear between the older pro-JCP Shingeki leadership and the younger theater people.

The differences manifested themselves in a number of ways: for one thing, the young people were disappointed by the lack of aggressiveness that the Shingeki leadership, in conjunction with the JCP, displayed in their leadership of the political demonstrations. The JCP and Shingeki leadership, for their part, roundly condemned such violent incidents as the student-led storming of the Diet on November 27, 1959 (which resulted in 12,000 people singing and snake dancing in the Diet Compound for three hours) and the sit-in at Haneda airport on January 15, 1960 intended to block the flight of Prime Minister Kishi to the United States to sign the Security Treaty. There were also more specific political differences: whereas the JCP was firmly tied to the party line given out by the Soviet Union and thus was prone to radical shifts

---

[19]The information on the involvement of Zengakuren in the AMPO struggle was taken from Stuart J. Dowsey, ed. Zengakuren: Japan's Revolutionary Students (Berkeley, CA: The Ishi Press, 1970). The two most useful chapters were Matsunami Michihiro, "Origins of Zengakuren" and Harada Hisato, "The Anti-AMPO Struggle."

in policy because of changes in Soviet leadership, the Zengakuren leadership called for a more non-aligned status, whereby the JCP would try to adjust its policy to the particular circumstances prevalent in Japan. In a 1980 interview with David Goodman (scholar and often active participant in the theater avant garde of the 1970's), Suzuki Tadashi, one of the foremost directors in Japan today, described the position taken by young theater people at the time:

> From the younger generation's point of view, the alternative proposed by the Old Left, principally the Japanese Communist Party (JCP), merely substituted an alliance with the Soviet Union for the existing relationship with the West. The young activists found the prospect of an alliance with the Soviet Block at least as repugnant as the alliance with the West, however.[20]

It was thus the feeling that Shingeki was unable to deal meaningfully with the concerns of contemporary postwar Japan, exacerbated during the 1960 anti-AMPO struggle by frustration with the subservience of the Shingeki establishment to Japanese Communist Party discipline that led to a radical break between the young and the old in theater.

Western dance in Japan, on the other hand, had never been as overtly political as Shingeki, and in fact, by the mid-50's was well on its way to becoming entrenched as just one more cultivated art that young, upper-middle class women were expected to learn before they married. With few political ties and little interest in dealing with the contemporary political concerns of young Japanese, the Western dance establishment in Japan left itself open much earlier than Shingeki to attack by the more radical and innovative elements in its midst, dancers who were interested in freeing dance from the yoke of Western cultural dominance. Thus it was that the beginnings of the Butō movement were laid long before the Security Crisis of 1960, in the experiments that Ohno and Hijikata worked on, both together and separately in their studios. The culmination of these experiments came with Forbidden Colors, which is now seen as the seminal work in the development of the Butō aesthetic. In 1960, when younger theater people as well as dancers were becoming politically and culturally disaffected with the West, Ankoku Butō was already there to present them with a persuasive alternative philosophy of theatrical expression.

---

[20] As quoted in David Goodman, "Satoh Makoto and the Post-Shingeki Movement in Japanese Contemporary Theatre" (Ph.D. diss., Cornell University, 1982), p. 18.

The Historical Context of Traditional Theater

One would naturally expect that the avant garde's antagonism towards the West would have led them to reconsider the indigenous dance theaters of Kabuki and Nō. However, the traditional forms of Kabuki and Nō, at least as they were perceived by the Japanese avant garde of the late 1950's, were in their own way felt to be just as stultifying and oppressive as Western dance and theater forms. The program notes for a performance by Bishop Yamada with the Butō troupe Hoppō Butō-ha in Hokkaido, clearly indicates the attitude of most Butō dancers: "By denying all that are dead: Kabuki, Nō, Classical Ballet...my journey begins, confirming the full unfolding of the body in new freedom...."[21] And as theater critic and director Tsuno Kaitarō has said in a different but related context: "Nō and Kabuki appear to us today as hollow forms. They have lost touch with the popular imagination that created them and that would enable them to grow."[22]

In fact, however, although Nō had left its plebian origins behind more that 500 years before to become an elite theatrical form exclusively patronized by the upper echelons of society, Kabuki theater had, up until the Meiji Restoration, been very much a theater of the masses. The style of Kabuki, especially the late-Edo period[23] plays that depicted the lower stratum of city life (kizewamono), clearly reflected its name's derivation from the archaic verb "kabuku," which literally meant "off-kilter," "skewed," or "perverse": to be called kabuku one had to be at the very forefront of fashion and art.

The evisceration of Kabuki occurred after the Meiji Restoration of 1868, as a result of a desire on the part of the new political leadership to find some indigenous performance art that they could transform into a "refined

---

[21]Bishop Yamada, program notes for a performance in Hokkaido, June 1979. The style of Yamada's name here is an exception to the rule I gave in footnote #1 (family name, given name); perhaps because Yamada has taken an English word for his given name in the theater, he is usually referred to according to the Western convention for names (given name, family name).

[22]Tsuno, "The Tradition of Modern Theatre," p. 10-11. This article addresses the question of why, for most postmodern dramatists in Japan, "the very theatrical forms that have appeared as alternatives to Western dramatists are not available to us" (p. 13).

[23]The Edo period began with the establishment of the Tokugawa shogunate in 1603, and ended with the Meiji Restoration of 1868.

theater that might be compared to the 'civilized' theater of Europe."[24] Leonard Pronko, in his article "Kabuki Today and Tomorrow," describes how in February of 1872 the leading Kabuki actors and writers in Tokyo were summoned to the prefectural office where they were informed that illustrious Japanese and foreigners, who were just then beginning to attend performances, might be offended by the overripe decadence of the late-Edo theater, and that the actors and writers should therefore do their best to raise the moral standards of Kabuki. This reprimand was taken very seriously by those involved in theater, and can be seen as the beginning of the end for Kabuki's participation in popular Japanese culture. As Pronko points out, it was from this time on that every effort was made to replace "the eroticism, flamboyance and fantasy of a theater that was a feast for the total spectator" with "a polite Sunday School picnic inspired by the 'tasteful' products of Victorian Europe."[25] Kabuki never recovered from this dose of Western puritanism; as it existed in the 1960's it was still, for all intents and purposes, the same sanitized variant of Kabuki that had been introduced almost a 100 years before to cater to upper class Japanese and Western notions of good taste. In other words, it had already been enervated by the very Westernization process that Ohno and Hijikata were attempting to transcend, and therefore in its contemporary form was no help to them at all.

One avenue that Butō has followed in their efforts to overcome the pernicious effects of Westernization on both contemporary and traditional dance/theater has been a nostalgic return to the primitive roots of dance, to a premodern (i.e. pre-Western influence) mode whose expressive power was to be derived from its links to the uncanny and irrational, to a kind of subterranean reservoir of raw sexual energy tied up in the intimate relation that primitive humanity once had with nature. This is the path that early experiments by Hijikata and Ohno followed, especially in the cathartic violence of Forbidden Colors and other dances of the early 60's based on ritual sacrifices, that culminated in Hijikata's most famous work, Hijikata Tatsumi to Nihonjin--Nikutai no Hanran (Hijikata Tatsumi and the Japanese --Revolt of the Flesh, 1968). It has been continued in the work of dancers like Tanaka Min, whose ecstatic trance improvisations are often danced to the pounding beat of live African-influenced jazz drumming, or Ojima Ichirō, whose solo dances are set in prehistoric ruins in order to participate in and communicate with the traces of aura left behind by prehistoric peoples.

---

[24]Tsuno, "The Tradition of Modern Theater," p. 10.

[25]Leonard Pronko, "Kabuki Today and Tomorrow," Comparative Drama 7 (Summer, 1972), pp. 103-104.

Finally, one can see it in the work of the Butō group Sankai Juku, founded by Amagatsu Ushio in the late 1970's. Although Sankai Juku's performances are not generally improvised, through their focus on primitive forms of life they attempt to reach the level of the collective unconscious and thus achieve cosmic significance for their art.

A second avenue of exploration was a revival of interest in the popular origins of Kabuki and Nō, along with a reassessment of early 20th century forms of popular theater, particularly the Asakusa "opera" (a kind of musical theater whose style incorporated both traditional and Western influences), Misemono (a form of theater that included acts comparable to a circus side show), and the Yose theater (similar in form to a vaudeville review centering on a comic monologue), all of which the critic Donald Richie has pointed out as formative influences on postwar avant-garde theater.[26] Such entertainments moreover, were themselves rooted in performative traditions that had existed prior to the emergence of Nō and Kabuki. In a sense both Nō and Kabuki could be said to have a common origin in some forerunner of Yose theater's loosely structured format of dance (usually erotically suggestive if not downright indecent), dramatic skits, and short comic monologues. Nō as we know it today began in the 14th century when Kanami borrowed the kusemai dance from the dancer/prostitutes who performed in the river beds of Nara and Kyoto; Kabuki traces its beginnings to a 15th century temple dancer/prostitute named Izumi no Okuni, who was famous for her scandalous takeoffs on well known figures of the day. However although Yose theater and forms like it had a long history, they only truly came into their own as the theater of the masses in the late 19th century, when the Kabuki theaters moved out of the slums of Asakusa, back towards the center of the city.[27] This move signalled Kabuki's new status as a purveyor of "civilization and enlightenment" to the upper classes, as well as the fact that they were leaving their lower class audience behind. In the void that was left with Kabuki's elevation to high culture, the Misemono and Yose theater flowered as the major forms of entertainment for the masses. Here is a description of what it was like in and around the precincts of the Kannon Shrine in Asakusa,

---

[26]Donald Richie, "Japan's Avant-garde Theater," The Japan Foundation Newsletter 7 (April-May 1979), p. 2.

[27]About 25 years before the Restoration, the Kabuki theaters were forced to move to the Northeastern fringes of Tokyo, just beyond Asakusa, near the Yoshiwara pleasure quarters. This had the effect of making Asakusa, particularly the area around the popular Asakusa Kannon Temple, the gateway to the theater and Yoshiwara districts.

according to Basil Hall Chamberlin and W.B. Mason's 1891 edition of their guide to Japan:

> ...nothing is more striking that the juxtaposition of piety and pleasure, of gorgeous altars and grotesque ex-votos, of pretty costumes and dingy idols...Here are raree shows, penny gaffs, performing monkeys, cheap photographers, street artists, jugglers, wrestlers, life-sized figures in clay, vendors of toys and lollipops of every sort, and circulating amidst all these cheap attractions, a seething crowd of busy holiday makers.[28]

Butō, and the theatrical avant garde influenced by Butō, saw these popular entertainments as the only legitimate heir of Kabuki and strove to incorporate their hurlyburly, riotous atmosphere. In the Yose theater's ribald, Rabelaisian humor and fantasy, as well as in the lower-class, marginal status of its actors, Hijikata hoped to find the energy and creative freedom lacking in the staid respectability of Kabuki in its 20th century form. The Butō groups Dai Rakuda-kan (Big Camel Battleship) and Dance Love Machine are well known for this style of Butō: their stages are filled not only with the detritus of early 20th century culture but with a hodgepodge of previous century's trash as well. The success of their attempt to recreate the energy of that period can perhaps be measured by a comment by the dance/drama critic Ichikawa Miyabi: "Dai Rakuda-kan has more of the essence of Kabuki than what Kabuki is today."[29]

The 1960's

Influences are notoriously difficult to trace, but at the very least it is safe to say that the unusual vision of Hijikata and Ohno contributed importantly to the "zeitgeist" of the early 1960's, the period of creative ferment that produced most of today's major avant-garde figures. During the years from 1960 to 1966, while the group Ankoku Butō-ha was still in existence, numerous dance performance collaborations between Ohno, Hijikata and the members of Ankoku Butō-ha were held. To mention a few among many:[30]

---

[28]As quoted in Edward Seidensticker, Low City, High City (New York: Alfred A. Knopf, 1983), p. 158.

[29]As quoted in "A Taste of Japanese Dance in Durham," New York Times, Sunday, 4 July 1982, Arts and Leisure section.

[30]This performance chronology was taken from a biographical "vita" given to me by Ohno Kazuo in November 1985.

there was the performance in 1960 in which Hijikata directed Ohno in the role of the old male prostitute, Divine, in a dance based on Genet's Notre Dame des Fleurs; in 1961 there was Hanin-hanyosha no Hirusagari no Higi (The Secret Daytime Ritual of an Hermaphrodite); in 1963, Anma--Aiyoku o Sasaeru Gekijo no Hanashi (The Blind Masseur--A Theatrical Story in Support of Love and Lust); in November of 1965 there was a joint memorial performance of Bara Iro Dansu (A Rose-Colored Dance) and in 1966 Ankoku Butō-ha formally broke up with a performance at Kinokuniya Hall of Tomato--Seiai Onchōgaku Shinanzue (Tomato--Introductory Lessons in the Blessed Teachings of Erotic Love). The incipient avant garde of the time not only saw these performances, they were also often active participants in them. For example, abstract painter Nakanishi Natsuyuki and graphic designer and illustrator Yokō Tadanori designed posters and sets for Ankoku Butō-ha productions. Nakanishi continued to influence Butō even after his collaborative efforts ended. In 1976, one of his abstract paintings inspired Ohno to create Admiring La Argentina and return to the stage again after ten years of semi-retirement. Yokō Tadanori was probably even more influential; he is usually given credit along with Hijikata for the "look" of not only Butō but also the avant-garde theater which was influenced by Butō. Like Hijikata, Yokō was interested in the popular culture of the early 20th century; drawing on the mass-produced popular art and advertising of the late-Meiji, Taisho, and early Showa period (approx. 1910-1930), Yokō's work was a "nostalgia" version of Pop Art. It may have lacked the cynicism of an Andy Warhol, but it was nevertheless resolutely set against the Japanese high culture's elitism and good taste. Donald Richie has described Yokō's and Hijikata's stage designs as representing,

> ...not only the end of the world but, especially, the end of Japan. The stage resembled a flea market and the effect was, purposely poignant. Here is the post-war wasteland, filled with spastic cripples holding aloft these pathetic emblems of vanished civilizations.[31]

Another important avant-garde figure influenced by Ankoku Butō was Terayama Shuji, the poet, playwright, and director who died in 1983 at the age of 47. Like Ohno and Hijikata, Terayama was born in the provincial Northern part of Japan (Tohoku). Before Terayama started Tenjō Sajiki, arguably the most important avant-garde theater group of the 1960's, he collaborated with Hijikata and Ohno on a number of scenarios for dances. In 1960 he participated in the second 650 Experience performance, which

---

[31]Richie, "Japan's Avant-Garde Theater," p. 2.

included a work based on the life of the Marquis de Sade: Sei Kōshaku (The Sainted Marquis). Like Hijikata, Terayama was antagonistic towards the high culture of Nō-Kabuki-Tea Ceremony, and looked instead towards the more popular culture of folk festivals and entertainments such as Misemono and Yose theater.

Kara Juro's work with Jōkyō Gekijō (Situation Theater) was also heavily influenced by Hijikata's preoccupation with the marginal elements of society, as well as his interest in the darkness of existence (which Kara called "yami" or "gloom"). The strongest link between the two was Maro Akaji, who studied with Hijikata at the same time that he was a major box office attraction for Kara's Jōkyō Gekijō. In the early 60's there wasn't a strong distinction made between what was theater and what was dance, and Kara, Maro, and Hijikata were very close. Eventually Maro left Jōkyō Gekijō to form Dai Rakuda-kan, and Kara's work became more political, as well as more overtly theatrical.

Finally there is Suzuki Tadashi, who as director of the Suzuki Company of Toga (SCOT) is probably the most familiar to the Western theatrical avant-garde. Suzuki was influenced by the search for a truly "Japanese" identity that was such an important element of the zeitgeist of the early to mid-60's. This influence came to fruition in the 70's with Trojan Women, in which Suzuki has been said to run through the whole history of Japanese theatrical styles, from Sarugaku (an early form of No) up through Shimpa, within the loose framework of the play by Euripides. This play marks the beginning of Suzuki's interest in reexamining the similarities between Japanese Nō theater and Classical Greek theater, the focus of most of his work in the last fifteen years. Hijikata's strong emphasis on the material nature of the body as the fundamental element in all performance was also taken up by Suzuki. He began to develop, at about the same time as Butō groups of the 1970's such as Sankai Juku, a vocabulary of movements that were based on kata (movement patterns) from Nō, Kabuki, and the martial arts.

In the dance world, the energy and charisma of Ohno and Hijikata, as well as their avant-garde stance, attracted a number of talented young people such as Kasai Akira, Maro Akaji (the founder of the Butō group Dai Rakuda-kan), Bishop Yamada (who formed the Grand Camellia School), Nakajima Natsu (founder of Muteki-sha), and Tanaka Min (mainly known as a solo dancer, but who recently formed a group called Maijuku), all of whom were restless and discontented with the state of dance in Japan at that time. Not all of these dancers actually studied under Hijikata or Ohno, but all of them have admitted to being strongly influenced in their own work by the Butō aesthetic. Both Ohno and Hijikata encouraged these dancers to go out and start their own companies, and by the mid-70's they had in turn spawned a third generation of smaller, more regional troupes, including Hoppō Butō-ha and Suzuran-tō (from Bishop Yamada's Grand Camellia School), Dance Love Machine and Amagatsu Ushio's Sankai Juku (from Maro Akaji's Dai Rakuda-kan).

Sankai Juku, although not the first Butō group to visit the United States (Ohno performed at La Mama in New York City in 1980, Dai Rakuda-kan at the American Dance Festival in Durham, North Carolina in 1982; Sankai Juku's first U.S. performance was at the Olympics Dance Festival in Los Angeles, 1984), has certainly provoked the most overwhelming critical response, and so can legitimately be said to have brought Butō to the attention of the mainstream dance world. Sankai Juku is a good example of the Japanese phenomenon of gyaku-yunyū ("go out and come back"): Japanese artists often only achieve recognition at home in Japan after they have achieved recognition abroad. A determining factor in Sankai Juku's commercial success is undoubtedly the fact that the group is based in Paris rather than Tokyo, and gave their first major performances in Europe. However, critics who have watched Butō from the very beginning have strong reservations about Sankai Juku's work: they claim that in Sankai Juku much of the original innovative excitement and energy of Butō has been schooled and domesticated. It is often the case with avant-garde movements that when they become popular, they also become institutionalized, and in fact, for young dancers today Butō seems to have become merely one more method that it is necessary to learn, along with ballet and Western modern dance. The peak of the Butō movement's expansion was probably in the mid-70's (at that time there were 20 to 25 groups practicing it across Japan). Today there are almost no new groups being formed, although at the time of his death Hijikata was collaborating with Tanaka Min on a new dance form called Ren'ai (Love), which he hoped would infuse a more positive energy and life into Butō.[32]

Ohno Kazuo himself has objected to the use of the term "Ankoku Butō" in regard to his current work, explaining that he feels the term has become too confining: "I am a human being, I'm a dancer. That's all."[33] For much the same reasons, such New York-based Japanese artists as Eiko and Koma, who in the early 1970's worked for a very short time (two months) with

---

[32]The Ren'ai style was shown to the public for the first time in September 1981 in a dance called Foundations, performed by Tanaka Min and held on the occasion of Tanaka's 1500th solo performance.

[33]As quoted in Marie Myerscough, "Butō Special," Tokyo Journal 4 (February 1985), p. 8.

Hijikata Tatsumi, and a relatively longer time (two years in total) with Ohno Kazuo, object strongly to critical categorization of their work as "Butō." Nowadays, the word Butō has come to share the very same stigma that it had originally attempted to transcend: as the movement has become stronger and more influential, paradoxically it has begun to lose its ability to escape categorization and interpretation. Witness the critical success, both in Japan and in the United States, of Kisanuki Kuniko (designated "Japan's Dancer of the Year, 1984" by the Japan Dance Critic's Association), who alternated performances with Ohno Kazuo at the Joyce Theater in New York City in November 1985. Kisanuki's training has included ballet, modern dance, and Butō, and although visually and structurally her work incorporates many of Butō's techniques, her sheer technical virtuosity glosses every movement with a sleek beauty that belies Butō's original aesthetic.

Butō as a Postmodern Dance Form

Although traditional forms as they existed in the 20th century were deemed sterile and unable to cope effectively with the contradictions and anxieties of contemporary life, there were a number of compelling reasons for the avant garde to look again at some of traditional dance theater's techniques and principles. For one thing, as dance forms unique to Japan, with extremely long histories (Nō goes back more than 600 years), it would be expected that they had evolved a vocabulary of movement eminently suitable to the Japanese body structure;[34] a second point in their favor was that the codes of representation on which Japanese dance theater is based are in many ways the antithesis of the Western theatrical model, and could therefore be used to confront and transcend it.

---

[34]It is not, in fact, clear to me that the structure of the Japanese body is significantly different from a German or American body, or that modern dance and ballet training is any more "natural" for an American than it is for a Japanese. Considering the number of Americans who are either members of a Butō troupe or have trained with one, the repeated references in the literature about Butō to the founders' desire to create a dance form particularly suitable for the Japanese physique should probably be taken with a grain of salt. One might consider however, the pervasive notion (only very recently challenged) that the Japanese body is unsuitable for classical ballet and modern dance. Although Hijikata's claim to have created a style of dance specifically for the Japanese body may not have been realistic, it was certainly ideologically persuasive, and must be taken into account on that basis.

As a result, Butō choreographers had no compunction about regarding these traditional dance forms as a kind of treasure trove of technique, gesture, and principles, which could be appropriated without regard to their original context or meaning, stripped down, and transformed into kata (a vocabulary of movement patterns). These kata could then be combined and recombined to form a dance idiom they felt would be more suitable for the Japanese body. In fact, in this regard, the vocabulary of movements upon which Nō and Kabuki are based were supposedly given no more weight than any of the other East and Southeast Asian dance traditions--everything was ripe for the plucking--the result of this pastiche method being a dance "technique" in which can be seen glimpses of everything from Kathakali hand gestures to the Chinese martial art of Tai Chi Chuan.

Although many of these movements and gestures had quite specific meanings within their own traditional context, those meanings were stripped away in the appropriation process, becoming unintelligible (or unreadable) to the viewer. This lines up with the fact that although the metaphorical load in a work may be quite heavy, most Butō choreographers strenuously resist any interpretation or explanation of individual gestures or techniques as having some concrete, easily identifiable meaning or reference. Nakajima Natsu of Muteki-sha is typical when she states in her program notes, "The gestures do not tell a story but evoke associations--to explain a movement is to undermine its meaning."[35] Amagatsu Ushio of Sankai Juku put it another way when he said that he is satisfied if "the performance serves as a spark for the feelings within the bodies of the individuals watching it."[36]

Butō's pastiche style, which picks and chooses among modern and premodern dance techniques, elite and popular forms, with little or no regard for their original context or meaning certainly accords well with Frederic Jameson's characterization of the postmodern as "the random cannibalization of all styles of the past, the play of random stylistic allusion."[37] In fact, there are a number of parallels between the Butō aesthetic and the model for a postmodern art outlined by Jameson in his recent article, "Postmodernism, or the Cultural Logic of Late-Capitalism." To begin with, Hijikata's celebration of the carnivalesque atmosphere of the "low" culture of 19th century

---

[35]Program notes for Niwa (The Garden), performed by Muteki-sha at The Asia Society, New York City, September 28 and 29, 1985.

[36]Oyama, "Amagatsu Ushio," p. 71.

[37]Frederic Jameson, "Postmodernism, or The Cultural Logic of Late-Capitalism," New Left Review, no. 146 (July-August 1984), pp. 65-66.

Kabuki as well as elements of Taisho mass culture corresponds to the postmodern effacement of "the older (essentially high-modernist) frontier between high culture and so-called mass or commercial art" through an avocation of the "whole 'degraded' landscape of schlock and kitsch."[38] Jameson associates this technique of random cannibalization with what he calls "the Nostalgia mode," the attempt to "lay siege either to our own present and immediate past, or to a more distant history that escapes individual existential memory,"[39] and he uses the movie American Graffiti (1973) as an example to demonstrate that, "for Americans at least, the 1950's remains the privileged lost object of desire."[40] The Nostalgia mode is quite clearly at work in Butō; as mentioned earlier, not only were there members of the Butō movement who were nostalgic for the vital energy of early 19th century popular forms (uncontaminated by Western culture) and the kitsch of early 20th century mass-produced art, but there were also members of the Butō movement who looked back much further, to a "world of darkness that our modern age has lost, where the gap between words and things disappears and where existence unfolds before us."[41] Read through Freud, this latter attempt appears to be the purest possible example of the postmodern nostalgia for "the privileged lost object of desire": a desire to regress to the pre-oedipal period of childhood, "a time when," as Freud says, "the ego was not yet sharply differentiated from the external world and from other persons."[42] Actually, the very fact that Butō finds itself dispersed among three forms of nostalgia--the popular culture of the carnivalesque, the familiar vulgarity of kitsch, and the primal longings for childhood--is itself a marker of its postmodern condition: Butō plays randomly across the various fields of desire in the individual and collective history, picking and choosing with no care for any apparent contradiction.

Butō can also be considered postmodern in its desire to displace "those canonical experiences of radical isolation and solitude, anomie, private revolt, Van Gogh-like madness, which dominated the period of high

---

[38]Jameson, "Postmodernism," pp. 54, 55.

[39]Jameson, "Postmodernism," p. 67.

[40]Jameson, "Postmodernism," p. 67.

[41]Eguchi Osamu, "Hoppō Butō-ha 'Shiken' " (My View of Hoppō Butō-ha), Butōki, no. 2 (1980), p. 9. Page numbers cited hereafter refer to translation in appendix. For this citation see p. 90.

[42]Sigmund Freud, "The 'Uncanny,' " trans. Alix Strachey, in Studies in Parapsychology, ed. Philip Rieff (New York: Collier Books, 1977), p. 42.

modernism."[43]   In this, Butō follows the general shift in the dynamics of cultural pathology from the celebration of the alienated, isolated artist, to a celebration of the fragmented, schizophrenic artist. I will return to this point in more detail in the next chapter; however, I should note here that in contradistinction to Jameson's characterization of both the use of pastiche and the emphasis on the fragmentation of self as tending to be purely aesthetic and formal, with no wider social or political goals involved,[44] Butō's use of those forms should be seen as part of an overall strategy that aims at the ultimate reunification of the self into an all-encompassing order of nature.

Finally, Butō can be seen as postmodern in its antagonism towards critical interpretation. Jameson uses E.L. Doctorow's The Book of Daniel as an example of the postmodern resistance to critical interpretation; the practitioners of Butō, like Doctorow, have structured their work, "systematically and formally to short-circuit an older type of social and historical interpretation which it perpetually holds out and withdraws."[45] Butō dancers use various strategies besides pastiche to achieve this goal, including a stress on grotesque imagery and the use of metamorphosis; I will return to this point in more detail in the next chapter.

---

[43]Jameson, "Postmodernism," p. 63.

[44]Jameson explains that although parody had an "ulterior motive" in its satiric impulse, the pastiche form which has supplanted it in postmodern practice is a "neutral practice" and thus has become a "blank parody, a statue with blind eyeballs." Jameson, "Postmodernism," p. 65.

[45]Jameson, "Postmodernism," p. 69.

Chapter Two

THE BUTŌ AESTHETIC AND A SELECTION OF TECHNIQUES

The Butō Aesthetic

The Butō aesthetic has evolved a great deal in the last twenty-five years; although many of the fundamental principles of the Butō movement were first expressed in Forbidden Colors, it is unlikely that the wildly enthusiastic audience for Sankai Juku would have reacted similarly to Hijikata's debut work. The aesthetic revealed in Forbidden Colors was not only adverse to technique, it was also dead set against giving the audience a pleasurable experience. In fact, Donald Richie has described Hijikata's early works as all too often being "distinguished by their length, their apparent irrationality, [and] their intended boredom...."[1] One of Ankoku Butō's original aims was the exploration of the submerged depths of violence and sexuality, but at the same time it attempted to suppress the symbolic expression of ordinary emotions through dance; it discarded music and interpretive program notes; it dealt explicitly with the socially taboo topic of homosexuality. All in all it is not surprising that Ankoku Butō was primarily an underground performance art throughout most of the 1960's.

The movement existed underground in the literal sense as well: it was in the tiny, informal, basement theater-cafes of Tokyo, playing to a converted audience of relatives and friends, that Butō flourished. As the movement expanded and dancers broke off to form new groups, many of the original goals were modified, refined in various ways reflecting the tastes of the individual choreographers. Thus it is that today an art that began as a movement towards minimalism is now often labelled expressionistic; music has once again become an essential element, and interpretive program notes for recent performances have occasionally looked more like magazine articles. A dance form that was violent and virulently set against giving the

---

[1]Richie, "Japan's Avant-garde Theatre," p. 2.

25

audience pleasure is now peaceful and aesthetically appealing; artists who disavowed technical virtuosity have themselves developed a whole series of techniques; an art that tried to distort, warp, and torture the body in order to keep the self in a constant state of fragmentation, now visualizes the body as "a cup filled to over-flowing, one that cannot take even one more drop of liquid," in order to help it enter "a perfect state of balance."[2] This development over time of a diversity of aims and ideals makes it impossible to define an overall Butō aesthetic, except as a loosely held group of attitudes about what dance should be. Ohno Kazuo, for example, who was a major figure in the origination of Butō, has remained on his own unique path, refusing to let his work fall into easy categories. He retains the original "anti-technique" bias of Butō, and therefore objects to many of the techniques that are described in the following sections, feeling that they are too limiting. For instance, he categorically rejects the characteristic Butō crouch, called ganimata, as focussing too one-sidedly on the depths below: "In life mustn't one look upwards as well?"[3] But Ohno's approach is that of a superbly original master who can depend on his enormous personal skill and his charisma on stage, an approach that cannot really be taught. His school in Yokohama is more of a place for Ohno to expound on his deep intellectual and spiritual commitment to the possibilities inherent in dance, than an institution established to teach "how to do Butō." It must also be kept in mind that for any one technique practiced by a particular Butō group, it is always possible to find another group that rejects it, or who may have developed some other technique that has a completely opposite goal. Even the white body makeup, considered such a distinctive feature of the "look" of Butō, was spurned by Tanaka Min and replaced by black or brown makeup in many of his solo dances.

Butō's Rejection of Technique and Use of the Grotesque

From the very beginning Hijikata and Ohno were opposed to technical virtuosity, interested in restricting the body to what it could do naturally, and resolutely set against the use of the body as an expressive tool. As Gōda Nario points out:

> In mainstream dance, pieces and scenes are constructed
> from the outside solely on the basis of a body that expresses
> itself externally, whereas Butō attempts to affirm the dance

---

[2]Amagatsu Ushio as quoted in Martin A. David, "Sankai Juku," High Performance 7, no. 3 (1985), p. 18.

[3]Ohno, interview with author, 1 July 1986.

which lies **within** the body--the body is, in itself, contemplated as a small universe--and its structure and performance are thus revitalized.[4]

In practice this restriction of dance to the body's concrete structure meant an eschewal of "realism," understood to mean any attempt to convey a story realistically through dance movements that mimed actions in the everyday world. It was also linked inseparably to an eschewal of "symbolism," which in practice meant an antagonism towards the sort of abstract, symbolic dance movements that the audience could interpret unequivocally as having a single set meaning. Nakajima Natsu, founder of the Butō group Muteki-sha, is typical when she states, "Butō should reject all formalism, symbolism and meaning by expressing our energy and freedom. I am striving, not towards art, but towards love."[5]

As an example of the kind of "symbolic" dance movement that Butō wishes to reject, Butō dancers often cite the kata in Nō drama called the shiori kata: when the shite (main character) raises its hand to face level, palm facing inward, it symbolizes that the character is crying.[6] Instead of this kind of highly stylized movement, which is seen as a gesture selected by a rational mind intent on portraying the emotion of grief in its most refined symbolic form, Butō dancers choose to stress the movement of the body in and of itself, unmotivated by any specific expressive intent. This point is made clearly by Eguchi Osamu in an essay on the Butō group, Hoppō Butō-ha:

---

[4]Gōda, "On Ankoku Butō," p. 86.

[5]As quoted in program from festival International de Nouvelle danse (Montreal, 19-29 September, 1985).

[6]This particular example was both mentioned to me by Ojima Ichirō in a personal interview, and is used in Iwabuchi Keisuke, "Butō no Paradaimu" (The Paradigm of Butō), Butōki no. 3 (1982), unpaginated. (Page numbers cited hereafter refer to translation in appendix. For this citation see pp. 74-5.) The fact is, however, that this kind of explicitly symbolic kata is actually the **rarest** of all the kata in Nō, since the majority of Nō kata have either no explicit symbolic meaning whatsoever (intended purely as a contribution to the total atmospheric effect of the piece), or whose symbolic meaning is completely relative, the same action (for example pointing upward with the fan) having a **number** of different meanings depending on the context of the play. This willful misunderstanding and discarding of Nō as merely "symbolic" was necessary, however, in order for Butō to be able to escape Nō's bonds, and be able to innovatively use other aspects of Nō principles and techniques.

28

Butō is like poetry in that it, in its very essence, resists the substitutive function in which words are used to express some **thing**. In poetry it is the words, in Butō it is the body- -the movement encloses within **itself** the extreme point which it must seek, while, at the same time, by twisting, jostling, and touching it opens up a symbolic space that enfolds both the reader and the spectator. Needless to say, within that symbolic space, any explanation which takes the form, "this means so-and-so" becomes meaningless.[7]

The action on stage is intended to be as resistant to critical interpretation, as multivalent and open as possible, in order to make possible a direct channel of communication between the audience and the dancer. It is hoped that this channel would be able to bypass the symbolic mode, which is seen as tainted by the inevitable intellectualizing process that traps both the viewer and the dancer in conventionalized perceptions. Ironically enough, in pursuit of their goal of creating dance that blocks critical interpretation, most practitioners of Butō gradually left their anti-technique bias behind and from the late 1960's on began to develop a whole range of specialized techniques. For example, the beshimi kata, in which the body convulses spasmodically, the eyes roll up to show the whites, the tongue spews out, and the face is twisted beyond all recognition, represents an attempt to move beyond the usual forms of expression to a level of grotesquery that would make it impossible to apply verbal explanations.

Grotesque imagery of this kind has become almost synonymous with the word "Butō." To understand why the grotesque should have taken on such an important role in the Butō aesthetic, we might turn for a moment to Geoffrey Galt Harpham's recent book, On The Grotesque. According to Harpham the grotesque, like metaphor, has the ability to hold multiple and conflicting interpretations in a kind of uneasy truce, so that "our understanding is stranded in a 'liminal' phase", with the result that, "Resisting closure, the grotesque object impales us in the present moment, emptying the past and forestalling the future."[8] Harpham uses "liminal" in its anthropological sense, to mean that the mind is caught "between two worlds" as it tries to understand rationally what its senses tell it is irrational.

---

[7]Eguchi, "My View of Hoppō Butō-ha," pp. 89-90.

[8]Geoffrey Galt Harpham, On the Grotesque: Strategies of Contradiction in Art and Literature (Princeton, NJ: Princeton University Press, 1982), pp. 14, 16.

In a passage strikingly similar to the passage from Eguchi's essay quoted above, Harpham goes on to compare the uses of the grotesque in art with that of metaphor in poetry and fiction:

> ...in the case of both metaphor and the grotesque, the form itself resists the interpretation that it necessitates. We remain aware of the referential absurdity of the metaphor despite our attempts to transcend it, and the discord of elements in the grotesque remain discordant....And because it calls forth contradictory interpretations to which it refuses to yield, it disrupts the relationship between art and the meaning of art.[9]

Harpham points out the affinity that artists who espouse an "art for art's sake" position feel for the grotesque: figures that "seem to be singular events, appearing in the world by virtue of an illegitimate act of creation, manifesting no coherent, and certainly no divine intention," are the perfect material for "'aesthetic' artists who insist on the non-mimetic character of artistic creation."[10] Thus Butō's landscape of distorted and commingled forms, half human, half "other," can be seen as an essential element in Butō's anti-symbolic/anti-realism stance, and as part of an overall strategy of blocking critical interpretation in an attempt to reach the audience on an physical ("gut") level.

Harpham, following Freud in Beyond the Pleasure Principle, characterizes the grotesque as a manifestation of the repressed unconscious, or id. In the grotesque's amorphous forms we see intimations of the id as it appears to the ego: that is, as "a chaos, a cauldron full of seething excitations."[11] When the id, in the concrete form of the grotesque, pierces into our consciousness we become aware of a distinct feeling of **repulsion**. I would go on to say that although we feel repulsed, there is at the same time a reluctant sense of identification: the grotesque, like the uncanny, "is nothing else than a hidden, familiar thing that has undergone repressing and then emerged from it...."[12] Butō exploits this relationship between grotesque images and the repressed unconscious in an effort to create a more direct line of communication

---

[9]Harpham, On the Grotesque, pp. 178-9.

[10]Harpham, On the Grotesque, p. 5.

[11]Sigmund Freud, Beyond the Pleasure Principle, as quoted in Harpham, On the Grotesque, p. 67.

[12]Freud, "The 'Uncanny,'" p. 51.

between dancer and spectator. Gōda Nario's description of his feelings while watching Forbidden Colors is a good example of how Butō creates its desired effect:

> It made those of us who watched it to the end shudder, but once the shudder passed through our bodies it resulted in a refreshing sense of release. Perhaps there was a darkness concealed within our bodies similar to that found in Forbidden Colors and which therefore responded to it with a feeling of liberation.[13]

Gōda's experience is a model illustration of the proper response to the use of the grotesque in Butō: his physical sense of repulsion leads to a dim feeling of identification which in turn triggers a sense of release. This liberation of man's "darker side, connected with the vulgar and possibly orgiastic growth processes in the depths"[14] is seen as the crucial first step towards bringing the "high" and "low" into balance, with the eventual goal of reintegrating man into nature.

However, while on one level it is the confused feeling of fascination and repulsion that the grotesque inspires that paralyzes our rationality, and allows this kind of physical communication to occur, on another level the discomfort we feel in the face of the inexplicable becomes the catalyst that sends us scrambling to find meaning, whether by trying to discover an overarching principle that we will be able to use to explain what we have seen, or by normalizing our experience by trying to find connections of resemblance to other better understood entities. This nearly inevitable desire to contain and categorize what we cannot understand stands in constant conflict with Butō's expressed goals, but as Harpham has so succinctly put it, "art lives by resisting interpretation as well as by inviting it...."[15] The fact that "the form itself resists the interpretation that it necessitates" goes a long way towards explaining why it is that a movement that was so set against critical interpretation is nevertheless beginning to generate a significant amount of critical writing, along with a great deal of metaphorical/poetic writing by the dancers themselves.

---

[13]Gōda, "On Ankoku Butō," p. 81.

[14]Harpham, On the Grotesque, p. 73.

[15]Harpham, On the Grotesque, p. 178.

Anti-Individualism and the Uses of Violence

In the literature surrounding Butō there are a number of references to the notion of the individual subject and its status in late-modern society. The antagonism exhibited in these writings towards the ideology of individualism has its history in both the early postwar Japanese intellectual and critical debate on subjectivity (shutaisei[16]) and later discussions, within the context of the 1960's AMPO crisis, about the relation between community and individual autonomy. Sakuta Keiichi, in an article that traces the history of the 1960's controversy over community and autonomy, describes how at that time there emerged in the thought of the "folk-nativist" faction of historians (historians who based much of their insights on the folklore studies, or Minzokugaku, of Yanagita Kunio) the view that submergence in community didn't necessarily prevent autonomy, but might rather be the basis for autonomy.[17] The folk-nativist historians, in line with Yanagita's views on Japanese village communities (buraku), called for a reassessment of the buraku as a potential locus of resistance versus centralized authority and therefore as a possible indigenous basis for a truly Japanese form of autonomy.

Although there are no concrete connections, the ideas of these folk-nativist historians and the resurgence of interest in the native ethnographic work of Yanagita Kunio were a pervasive cultural influence on artists in the 1960's, and Butō was no exception.[18] On a popular level, Yanagita's explora-

---

[16]For an analysis of the debate on shutaisei, see J. Victor Koschmann, "The Debate on Subjectivity in Postwar Japan: Foundations of Modernism as a Political Critique," Pacific Affairs, vol 54, no. 4 (Winter 1981-2), pp. 609-631. Koschmann points out in this article that a good deal of ambiguity surrounds the term shutaisei itself, and that a substantial part of the debate was simply an attempt to define the term. According to Koschmann, shutaisei came to mean not only "A form of subjectivity, authenticity, or 'selfhood,'" but it also connoted firm commitment to political action and a stance of independence or autonomy in relation to the potentially deterministic forces of history and social structure.

[17]Sakuta Keiichi, "The Controversy Over Community and Autonomy" in J. Victor Koschmann, ed., Authority and the Individual in Japan (Tokyo: Tokyo University Press, 1978), p. 240.

[18]The following description of Yanagita Kunio's work is based mainly on essays in J. Victor Koschmann, Ōiwa Keibō and Yamashita Shinji, eds., "International Perspectives on Yanagita Kunio and Folklore Studies," Cor-

tion of the oral traditions of the marginal mountain people (yamabito) and the people of the small local farming communities (jōmin) played on the nostalgia of the urban Japanese for their rural roots. In addition, the fact that Yanagita never quoted Western scholars, dealt only with Japan, and insisted on the unique character of Japanese institutions made his ideas very appealing to artists and intellectuals who had been alienated from the West by the AMPO struggle and were searching for an indigenous critical or revolutionary tradition.[19]

For Butō, the most influential aspects of Yanagita's thought were his desire to transcend the modern, with the corresponding antagonism towards the Western ideal of individualism; his interest in breaking through to a collective (or communal) unconscious in order to find a more authentic autonomy of self; and his preoccupation with marginal elements of Japanese society such as women, children, the insane, and the very old, whom Yanagita thought were the unconscious bearers of authentic Japanese tradition because of their structurally inferior position.[20]

Echoes of Yanagita's ideas appear again and again in the work and writings of Butō choreographers. Take for example some of the various techniques that Butō choreographers have developed in response to the problem of the individual subject. Shaving the head (a visual trademark of Butō that can be traced back to the shaved head of the influential German modern dancer Harald Kreutzberg) and coating the nearly naked body with white makeup eliminates all emblems of personal "taste," a step towards freeing the dancer from capitalism's consumer culture. Butō's use of continual metamorphosis to confront the audience with the disappearance of the individual subject by refusing to let any dancer remain a single identifiable character, is another strategy that challenges the modern myth of the individual. These techniques will be discussed separately in subsequent sections of this chapter; for now I wish to examine the role of violence in Butō,

---

nell East Asia Papers 37 (Ithaca, NY: China-Japan Program, 1985). Especially useful were Yamashita Shinji, "Ritual and 'Unconscious Tradition': A Note on About Our Ancestors"; J. Victor Koschmann, "Folklore Studies and the Conservative Anti-Establishment in Modern Japan"; and Bernard Bernier, "Yanagita Kunio's About Our Ancestors: Is it a Model for an Indigenous Social Science?"

[19]Bernier, p. 92.

[20]Yamashita, p. 62.

33

particularly with regard its use as a method to free the dancer (and the audience) from their belief in themselves as a unified subject.

The violence of works such as Forbidden Colors and Revolt of the Flesh originated in response to an assumption that continues to underlie all Butō: that in our modern society any attempt to maintain a sense of individuality, a sense of ourselves as a unified subject, is an effort doomed to failure. The critic Iwabuchi Keisuke sums up this belief: "if one neglects for even a moment the effort to maintain one's individuality, the pressure that our 'information society' (jōhō shakai) wields to force us into homogeneity will violate the individual, render him powerless, abandon, and eliminate him."[21] You might say that for Butō, the best defense is a good offence: since our sense of individuality is only a fragile delusion that could be exploded at any time, it is vital that we immediately begin to explore the possibility of our own inner fragmentation. If we can break through the bonds that have been embedded in our minds and conditioned deep into our bodies by our modern society, we may eventually gain access to our **real** self (what the critic Ichikawa Miyabi has called "the body that has been robbed"[22]). Butō's ritualized violence, with its overtones of primitive sacrifice, help Butō dancers to achieve this goal.

Our sense of ourselves as unified subjects is formed and supported by our unconscious acceptance of those social institutions (including language) which domesticate our more chaotic instincts, instincts that if let loose might play havoc with our belief in a unified rational self. This is one reason that the early experimentation of Ankoku Butō attempted to explore through dance the repressed unconscious of the individual: they hoped that by bringing out into the open those basic desires for violence and sexuality which challenge our everyday norms, the dancer would become aware of his own inner fragmentation, as the conflict between his deepest desires and his belief in his own rationality was made explicit. They were thus committed to, as Gōda Nario puts it, "the close examination of the relationship between existence and sexuality" by portraying on stage those manifestations of it that "come bursting forth from the abyss of darkness."[23] On stage these manifes-

[21]Iwabuchi Keisuke, "The Paradigm of Butō", p. 77.

[22]Ichikawa Miyabi, " 'Butō' Josetsu" (A Preface to Butō), in Butō: Nikutai no Suriarisuto-tachi (Butō: Surrealists of the Flesh), ed. Hanaga Mitsutoshi (Tokyo: Gendai Shokan, 1983), unpaginated. Page numbers cited hereafter refer to translation in appendix. For this citation see p. 71.

[23]Gōda, "On Ankoku Butō," p. 83.

tations of violence were at first directed towards animals such as the chicken in Forbidden Colors:

> In the dance motif of 'killing a chicken,' which Forbidden Colors and Revolt of the Flesh share, one could plainly see the turbulent passion of the boy's youthful flesh, an expression of a dark sexuality which he could neither control nor be set free from.[24]

With Revolt of the Flesh (1968) the violence began to be directed not only at external objects but at the self as well, a natural progression that was brought to fruition in the early 1970's in the dance of Hangi Daito-kan. Hangi Daito-kan was less a "group" than a concept: its work was based on the idea that "only by throwing off the body and transcending suffering can true dance be created, and that Butō **begins** with the abandonment of self."[25] Ichikawa Miyabi sees this self-directed anger as being the only possible response to a body whose every nook and cranny has been infiltrated by the social institutions of modernity.[26] It is only by abandoning the notion of the individual subject, and fragmenting the body through self-torture, that we can be released from the deeply imbedded social archetypes conditioned into every fiber of our bodies.

The Appropriation of Marginality

As mentioned in the first chapter, since the refined elegance of the fully developed forms of Nō and Kabuki, as practiced today, held no interest for Butō choreographers, they turned instead to the **popular** origins of classical theater in order "to use the premodern imagination as a negating force to transcend the modern."[27] Butō artists have been interested in appropriating the marginal, outcaste position of Japanese actors in general, but have been particularly interested in appropriating the position of Edo Kabuki actors, who were called kawara mono (riverside beggars), because in the early days they lived and performed on dried out riverbeds, the most temporary (therefore most marginal) of spaces in Edo Japan.

In an agrarian society, the nomadic life of entertainers is often viewed with suspicion; as outsiders, early Kabuki actors had a marginal status in

---

[24]Gōda, "On Ankoku Butō," p. 82.

[25]Gōda, "On Ankoku Butō," p. 85.

[26]Ichikawa, "A Preface to Butō," p. 70.

[27]Tsuno, "The Tradition of Modern Theater," p. 19.

Japanese society that theater anthropologists such as Yamaguchi Masao and Hirosue Tamotsu have seen as carrying on in the tradition of itinerant priests who travelled from village to village, enhancing their religious rituals and parables with various kinds of performances. Yamaguchi, who has written several articles on the intimate connection between marginality and theater, believes that originally Kabuki actors, like those itinerant priests, "were gods and sacrificial victims, sacred and polluted, visitors from a greater world and at the same time bearers of the sins of the community."[28] Hirosue, in an essay on Kabuki called, "The Secret Ritual of the Place of Evil," writes even more extravagantly that,

> For much of Japanese history bands of itinerant actor-prostitutes spiritually trespassed the country. As itinerant agents of the gods they would dominate the populace. Simultaneously, however, they were forced to relieve the people's suffering, taking their sins and imperfections upon themselves. They were thus as much scapegoats of men as they were the deputies of gods. Capable of impersonating the gods, they also had to shoulder the suffering of man. As Actors on stage they concentrated and purged sins and imperfections, even acting out man's detested death.[29]

By the late Edo period Kabuki actors could no longer truly be seen as 'scapegoat' figures, but Kabuki as an institution retained its unique position straddling the barrier between what was considered the inside and the outside of the Japanese social structure. It had taken on the role of mediator between those on the inside and those excluded categories of people such as burakumin,[30] geisha, the deformed, and diseased, who, by virtue of their exclusion, symbolically maintained the cultural order. Although like geisha, Kabuki actors weren't included in the four classes established by the Tokugawa

---

[28]Yamaguchi Masao, "Kingship, Theatricality, and Marginal Reality in Japan," in Text and Context, ed. R.K. Jain (Philadelphia: Institute for the Study of Human Issues, 1977), p. 173.

[29]Hirosue Tamotsu, "The Secret Ritual of the Place of Evil," Concerned Theatre Japan 2, no. 1 (1971), p. 20.

[30]Burakumin (literally, "hamlet people") is the modern name for the hereditary outcast group in Japan. They were originally discriminated against because they worked at occupations that in Buddhist terms were unclean, for example, leather working, street cleaning, or caretaking in cemeteries and crematoriums.

government (samurai, farmers, artisans and merchants), their position as outcastes did not subject them to the kind of unmitigated degradation and humiliation that the burakumin faced.[31] Instead, Kabuki actors shared with geisha a special status as outsiders: although they were forced to live separately and were not allowed to marry into the other classes they were, paradoxically, idolized by the populace and were the prime movers behind the Edo period taste in art and fashion.

Yamaguchi has explained this contradiction in anthropological terms: "while the Japanese, like other peoples, needed to reassure themselves of their own identities by excluding certain categories, they also felt a deep need to restore their relationships with these excluded categories, which were charged with metaphorical richness."[32] It was on the Kabuki stage that spectators could witness dimensions of human behavior that were normally excluded from their lives, but which, on some unconscious level, held great appeal and with which they deeply needed to identify. Kabuki, especially the late-Edo period style Kabuki called kizewamono, took the marginal spaces and figures of the Edo era and made them the central focus of their plots: the characters in Sakurahime (The Scarlet Princess of Edo), for example, included thieves, prostitutes, ex-priests defrocked for illicit sexual liaisons, even burakumin themselves; the settings included a cemetery, an execution ground, a burakumin village, a river bed, and a thieves' hideaway in the mountains.

Hijikata and the avant garde wished to appropriate from Kabuki its ability to slip between and through the cracks of the rigid Japanese social structure, seeing in its fluidity and its connection to the "outside" a potential source of creativity (what Gaston Bachelard in The Poetics of Space has

---

[31]The Tokugawa government (bakufu) instituted the four class system of samurai, farmers, artisans, and merchants, with the aristocracy above and the outcasts below. Yamaguchi has elaborated this schema by placing actors and geisha outside the four classes but above the burakumin group. It was only with this class structure's codification into law that being an outcaste became hereditary, as opposed to being the outcome of occupation: there eventually came to be quite a few burakumin farmers, fishermen, and weavers who were discriminated against on the basis of nothing other than their family heritage. For a summation of the evolution of the caste system in Japan, see Hane Mikiso, Peasants, Rebels and Outcastes (New York: Pantheon Books, 1982).

[32]Yamaguchi Masao, "Theatrical Space in Japan, a Semiotic Approach," unpublished manuscript. I am indebted to Prof. Brett de Bary for letting me have a photocopy of this manuscript.

termed "the raw materiality of the possibility of being"[33]), as well as a possible vehicle for social criticism. They also sought to incorporate Kabuki's intimate connections to the dark, taboo, repressed side of everyday life, and hoped that by taking on Kabuki's role of representing all that was seemingly unrepresentable in Japanese society, they might also appropriate Kabuki's "particularly provocative technique of converting the socially negative into the aesthetically positive."[34] To do so they strove to bring into their dance the original meaning of Kabuki, which Tsuno Kaitarō has defined as that which "implies the destruction of our everyday sensory balance through grotesque, comic and exaggerated posturing."[35] As mentioned in the first chapter, because they felt that Kabuki and Nō had been enervated by their respective elevations to high culture, they also turned to Asakusa vaudeville as the 20th century equivalent of Kabuki's original atmosphere of the carnivalesque.

In order to return to either of these "origins" of dance, Butō has had to tread a difficult line, the line that kept this faintly nostalgic, romantic attitude towards folk or popular forms of traditional culture from disintegrating into the kind of uncritical idealization of "pure" Japanese values that in the prewar period was used so effectively by the right-wing military--an all too real possibility considering the path that Hijikata's good friend Mishima Yukio took. Mishima's desire to regain the purity of a mythical Japanese past certainly had an effect on Butō's development, particularly with regard to the revival of interest in indigenous theatrical forms. It may be that he had a political effect on some Butō groups as well; according to journalist Yoshida Teiko, dances performed by Maro Akaji's Dai Rakuda-kan in the 1970's occasionally incorporated sections that exhibited a Mishima-style neo-romantic militarism.[36]

Metamorphosis Exercise

Butō's interest in the marginal characters of the Kabuki stage helps to explain the Butō emphasis on figures that are marginal not only to contemporary society, but to all places and times: characters such as children, the

---

[33]Gaston Bachelard, The Poetics of Space (Boston: Beacon Press, 1969), p. 218.

[34]Yamaguchi, "Theatrical Space," unpaginated.

[35]Tsuno, "The Tradition of Modern Theater," p. 10.

[36]Yoshida Teiko and Miura Masashi, conversation with author, 22 January 1986.

38

handicapped (blind musicians are especially prominent), the insane, refugees, the primitive savage, the very old, even scapegoat figures from other cultures (one section of a performance held by Bishop Yamada and Hoppō Butō-ha in Sapporo explored the myth of Prometheus). Those who are the least caught up in the toils of modern culture are seen as being the most in touch with the natural world and with the natural instincts. It also helps to explain why metamorphosis--the transformation of one's body and spirit into the body of another animal or person--should play such a major role in Butō training, since by becoming these marginal characters one comes to identify with their marginal position.

Some of the other uses of metamorphosis in Butō have been touched on elsewhere in this thesis: particularly its use as part of the effort to fight the ideology of individualism. Butō takes as a given the notion that, as Frederic Jameson says, "when you constitute your individual subjectivity as a self-sufficient field and closed realm in its own right, you thereby also shut yourself off from everything else and condemn yourself to the windless solitude of the monad, buried alive and condemned to a prison-cell without egress."[37] One of Butō's goals is to move beyond that prison cell. Recognizing, along with Peter Berger and Thomas Luckmann, that "the 'sane' apprehension of oneself as possessor of a definite, stable, and socially recognized identity is continually threatened by the 'surrealistic' metamorphosis of dreams and fantasies,"[38] Butō therefore skillfully exploits such surrealistic metamorphosis to help destroy the myth of the alienated individual, and replace it with a fragmented self, as the first step towards the ultimate goal of reintegrating man into the universe. The critic Ichikawa Miyabi has suggested that the metamorphosis that lies at the very heart of the Butō "spectacle" is based on "the dual personality, or constant metamorphosis, of various characters, so that eventually, as it becomes impossible to tell one person from another, the individual subject disappears altogether."[39] In this way the audience is forced to take the first steps towards an awareness of the fragility of their own sense of self-unity. For the dancer, on the other hand, Butō's use of metamorphosis helps restore "the body that has been robbed" in the process of socialization into modern society. One way this benefit is achieved is through the use of an improvisation exercise based on the idea of metamorphosis that Hijikata

[37]Jameson, "Postmodernism," p. 64.

[38]Peter Berger and Thomas Luckmann, The Social Construction of Reality (New York: Anchor Books, 1967), p. 98.

[39]Ichikawa, "A Preface to Butō," p. 71.

developed around 1968, and which since then has become an indispensable part of Butō training.

An actual exercise that novice dancers begin with was described to me by Ojima Ichirō, founder of Hoppō Butō-ha:

> When I was learning to dance with Bishop Yamada, I began by studying a rooster for many days. The idea was to push out all of the human insides and let the bird take its place. You may start by imitating, but imitation is not your final goal; when you believe you are thinking completely like a chicken you have succeeded.[40]

The main objective of this exercise is to exchange the "windless solitude" of the alienated individual for a sense of communion with nature, and to infuse the dancer's body with "a kind of magic that attempts to regenerate both man's sense of being alive, and the power of primitive life, through a return to man as the 'naked insect.'"[41] It is not the form of the animal or object that is important in this exercise, but how well one is able to experience what it would be like to be some other kind of being, whose "loveliness, gentleness, fierceness, and beauty...comes from nothing other than their ability to artlessly adapt themselves to natural laws."[42] According to Gōda, Hijikata wanted to "restore the body to its natural state" by having the dancers experience firsthand the principle that in nature, before an individual plant or animal can develop its own distinctive voice, it must begin by adapting itself to its place in the natural order. The lesson to be learned was that the unique subjective voice is not the result of self-assertion but the natural outcome of "knowing one's place."

Another related objective, mentioned to me by Ojima, is that by doing the exercise over and over for years, one begins to see that one has a greater affinity for some plants or animals over others. This is meant to provide one with a form of self-knowledge about one's fundamental nature, by bringing one closer to those instincts that are most basic. Ojima commented on this technique further:

> So you imitate an old woman and maybe find that you have a real affinity for that particular way of moving; by trying to be different people and things one comes to find which have

---

[40]Ojima Ichirō, interview with author, 10 July 1985 in Otaru, Japan.

[41]Iwabuchi, "The Paradigm of Butō," p. 77.

[42]Gōda, "On Ankoku Butō," p. 87.

the closest relationship to your heart and body, and in this
way one finds not only one's own style of dance, but one's
own way of being in the world.[43]

The choice of who or what one is transformed into is therefore seen
as quite critical, since it might have personal as well as public effects. Some
dancers come to be identified specifically with certain animal "characters":
Ohsuga Isamu and Hiruta Sanai, who founded the group Byakko-sha (White
Tiger Company) are well known for their respective portrayals of a mythical
Chinese tiger and a possessed Shinto priestess (miko). Byakko-sha itself
specializes in the depiction of various kinds of creatures, both natural and
supernatural, and their dances are accompanied by all kinds of live music,
including traditional shamisen.

The Metempsychosic Model of Time

By returning to premodern dance and dramatic forms, the Butō
dancers and choreographers were able to find an alternative to the Western
classical model of dramatic construction, with its emphasis on realistic
narrative based in the rationalism of cause and effect and the linear organization of time into a beginning, middle, and end. In breaking through the
bonds of Western rationalism, the Butō choreographers hoped to create for
a short time on stage a vision of a world which was the antithesis of the
modern--a vision that David Goodman has described as characterized by,

>...anti-linear time, by a dramatic world presided over by the
>collective imagination, and by "yami" ("the dark"). "Yami"
>is an endlessly repeating, constantly changing, shapeless
>form of time. Things are not orderly or predictable but as
>innumerable and conflicting as thoughts and images.[44]

In the mythical world of primitive thought there is no contradiction between
chaos and cyclical repetition, between constant change and absolute equiva-
lence:

>Perpetual metamorphosis is the central premise of mythic
>thought, which operates on the principle of the cosmic
>continuum. According to this principle, no realm of being,
>visible or invisible, past or present, is absolutely discontinu-

---

[43]Ojima, interview with author, 10 July 1985.
[44]Goodman, "New Japanese Theatre," p. 166.

ous with any other, but all equally accessible and mutually interdependent.[45]

The theater critic Yamamoto Kiyokazu has given another name to this premodern, ritualistic model of time and being: he calls it the "metempsychosic mode," a model of time in which "there is only process, which is cyclical and endless."[46] Webster's dictionary adds "transmigration" to the definition: "The passing of a soul after death into some other body; either human or animal."[47] Amagatsu Ushio's work with Sankai Juku provides us with a perfect example of the metempsychosic mode at work in Butō. Their dance, Jōmon Shō (Homage to Prehistory) cycles metaphorically through the prehistoric life process of undulating growth, sporadically set back by catastrophe; the continuous struggle to move upward to stand in the light is interspersed with inevitable falls back into darkness.

As would be expected, the characteristic mode of being within the metempsychosic mode is that of metamorphosis, the constant change of one form into another; the privileged form of expression is the metaphor, which allows one to go from one image to the next by means of apparent similarity or affinity, rather than by means of a causal relationship in linear time. The fragmentation of the body in motion leads to the fragmentation of time and space: in Revolt of the Flesh,

> Hijikata rejected our common sense notions of continuity, slicing through time and space. Western dances that are quite sensible, such as the polka or the waltz, appeared before us distorted and chopped up, in order to overturn our preconceived ideas.[48]

He did this by, "fragmenting motion into articulated movements that expressed precisely the temporary forms of each moment"; making no attempt to link these fragmented forms into anything that might encourage the audience to see linear continuity, he entrusted the dance to the simple accumulation of such movements.[49] Since as Frederic Jameson (following

---

[45]Harpham, On the Grotesque, p. 51.

[46]Yamamoto Kiyokazu, "Kara's Vision: The World as Public Toilet," Canadian Theatre Review, no. 20 (Fall 1978), p. 31.

[47]Webster's New Universal Unabridged Dictionary, 2d ed., s.v. "metempsychosis."

[48]Gōda, "On Ankoku Butō," p. 86.

[49]Gōda, "On Ankoku Butō," p. 87.

Lacan) points out, "personal identity is itself the effect of a certain temporary unification of past and future with the present before one,"[50] this disintegration of time into discreet moments, and the disavowal of temporal unity, can be seen as one more component of the Butō attempt to fragment the self. Butō asserts along with Jameson that "such active temporal unification is itself a function of language." Eguchi Osamu makes clear Butō's essentially antilanguage stance when he says, "Butō breaks through all verbal definitions and snatches the audience's sensibilities away to a state of nakedness."[51] Citing the work of Roland Barthes, Eguchi elaborates on how language, by means of the metaphoric function, imposes itself between man and nature as a kind of pseudo-nature that causes the user to forget that s/he is utilizing a conventional system of signification handed down by previous generations:

> Language, which comes into existence through a union of mutually interacting elements, depends on the fact that words are separated from things to be able to function more quickly and freely. Then the network of meaning, which is based on the metaphoric function, establishes itself as a kind of pseudo-nature--in a sense, it could be said that it is this network which rears the human being.[52]

Rather than attempt to communicate in a world where there is an arbitrary relationship between language and meaning that masquerades as natural, Butō wants to go back to a time when there was a **motivated** relationship between sign and signification, a "pre-Babel" world that Eguchi describes as "a world in which words and things had not yet been differentiated," where everything is simultaneous with everything else, and all hierarchical relations of value have been destroyed and replaced by a "mandala woven from words and resemblances which, as it whirls around, creates correspondences between all things."[53]

The metempsychosic mode can work on the level of the collective unconscious, as it does in Jōmōn Shō, exploring and releasing social archetypes that Butō dancers believe are conditioned deep into the body; or it can work on the level of individual history, working to reveal the deeply repressed subconscious of each person. Ohno Kazuo takes these two levels to be deeply

---

[50]Jameson, "Postmodernism," p. 30.

[51]Eguchi, "My View of Hoppō Butō-ha," p. 89.

[52]Eguchi, "My View of Hoppō Butō-ha," pp. 90.

[53]Eguchi, "My View of Hoppō Butō-ha," p. 90.

interpenetrating, as one can see in <u>Admiring La Argentina</u>, in which Ohno portrays his vision of the individual life as a microcosm of universal experience: "I had always read about the creation of the world in the Bible. I had always accepted it as legend, but in La Argentina's work I saw it realized in front of my eyes."[54] For Ohno the personal biography can only exist within a universal history, and within our individual memories there exists an "infinity of memories of past human lives."[55] The structure of the work reflects this attitude, **beginning** as it does with the last moments in the life of an old, old woman, who is then reborn in the **second** section in the form of a young girl. Ohno's work in <u>Admiring La Argentina</u> is also a good example of the fragmentation of Western-style dance modes: we might expect when Ohno comes on stage dressed in a flamenco costume and begins to dance to a tango, that we are going to see some kind of imitation "Spanish" dancing. What we see instead are tattered bits and scraps of familiar yet strangely unfamiliar movement swirled together into a whole that paradoxically seems both seamless and discordant. Ohno dismantles the structure of the flamenco before our very eyes, to reveal those emotions that were seminal in the **origins** of flamenco dancing. <u>Admiring La Argentina</u>, far from being an imitation, becomes a primal vision of flamenco's creation.

It seems to me that although neither the Butō choreographers nor the related theatrical avant garde mention it specifically, the metempsychosic mode has many thematic affinities with the aesthetic concept known as <u>jo-ha-kyū</u>, which is omnipresent in traditional Japanese theater. Western dramatic structure generally builds slowly and inevitably up to a **single** dramatic climax, which ends the work. In Japanese theater, on the other hand, the pacing cycles through a **series** of climaxes, each greater than the one before, until with the final and greatest climax we are suddenly returned to the level where we started.

As outlined in Monica Bethe and Karen Brazell's three volume work, <u>Dance in the Nō Theater</u>, <u>jo</u> is a slow, formal beginning, <u>ha</u> breaks this open and develops the theme, and <u>kyū</u> is the final release. The overarching structure of a Nō play moves from a slow, simple beginning (<u>jo</u>), progressively developing (<u>ha</u>) towards a high-powered, complex ending (<u>kyū</u>), which in turn gives way again to <u>jo</u>, in order to begin a new cycle for the next play. The pace of each of the dance sections that go to make up a Nō performance is itself

---

[54]As quoted in Jennifer Dunning, "Birth of Butō Recalled by Founder," <u>New York Times</u> (20 November 1985), p. C27.

[55]As quoted in Dunning, "Birth of Butō," p. C27. Additional information came from a personal conversation with Ohno, 24 November 1985.

governed by the rhythm of jo-ha-kyū; each has an internal movement from restraint to release, and then back to restraint. The areas of the stage are designated as jo-ha-kyū as well: the upstage third is considered jo, the middle third is ha, and the downstage third is kyū. And of course the pacing, rhythm, and level of complexity of the music in Nō are governed by jo-ha-kyū as well.[56]

It may be that in Butō's revolt against both Western and Japanese traditional theater, the aesthetic of jo-ha-kyū seemed too restricting and old-fashioned for them to claim for their own. On the other hand, it may be such a natural and unconscious part of theater and dance in Japan (Eugenio Barba claims that the three phases of jo-ha-kyū "impregnate the atoms, the cells, the entire organism of Japanese performance"[57]) that it does not need to be explicitly expressed. After all, the idea behind jo-ha-kyū is that asymmetrical, yet simultaneously cyclical rhythm is the natural rhythm of human life, that "the most natural way of being and doing is to begin slowly, gradually build to a climax, to stop and begin again."[58]

Although the structure of a Butō performance does not, of course, necessarily have to follow the pacing and structure of a Nō play, one can often see interesting parallels to it. In Butō, besides the similarity between the metempsychosic model of endlessly repeating time and the cyclical attitude toward time manifested in jo-ha-kyū, jo-ha-kyū is most clearly evidenced in Butō's pacing, especially in its constant movement back and forth between the poles of integration and disintegration: a stage filled with violence and chaos suddenly becomes a vision of idyllic, peaceful beauty, a vision which gives way in turn to a nightmare even more hellish than the one before.

An especially strong point of similarity is the way the opening dances in Butō nearly always correspond to the jo level prescribed for opening dances

---

[56]Monica Bethe and Karen Brazell, "Dance in the Nō Theater," Cornell East Asia Papers 29 (Ithaca, NY: China-Japan Program, 1982), vol. 1, p. 7-13; vol. 3, p. 188.

[57]Eugenio Barba, "Theater Anthropology," The Drama Review 26 (Summer 1982) p. 22. In this article Barba, who has been very interested in the possibilities for cross-cultural exchange of theatrical techniques between the East and West, explores certain recurrent principles (among them jo-ha-kyū) in the theatrical practice of East Asia, which he feels might be found useful by actors in the West.

[58]Komparu Kunio, The Noh Theater: Principles and Perspectives, trans. Jane Corddry and Steven Comee (New York, Weatherhill, 1983), p. 29.

in Nō. For an example of this, one has only to think of the famous first section in Sankai Juku's Jōmon Shō (Homage to Prehistory), in which four whitened, shaved, and nearly naked dancers were lowered upside-down from the proscenium by infinitesimal degrees; nothing could have captured our attention more completely. This was an act that seemed to literalize the "fall of the self," the moment in Zen when the very foundations of selfhood are shattered, and the analytic walls of interpretation collapse, allowing for an intuitive interpenetration into the world's true reality.[59] Another more recent example occurred in the performance of Tefu Tefu by Kisanuki Kinuko at the Joyce Theater in November of 1985. That dance began in complete darkness; it was only after a minute or two that we became aware of a single bluish spotlight shining from the level of the stage floor straight out into the audience. After a few minutes spent staring at that, we became aware that Kisanuki had appeared in our midst. She had entered from the rear of the theater, and was making her way down the aisle towards the stage by means of extraordinarily tiny steps; she looked like nothing so much as a moth hypnotized by the light that shone directly into her eyes (an appropriate image in a piece whose name means "butterfly").

These two examples of opening sections from Butō dances actually have exactly the same goal as the jo level god play has in Nō: that of capturing the audience's attention, while simultaneously putting them into the kind of mood that would be most conducive to appreciating the rest of the performance. The minimal movement in these opening pieces creates a sense in the viewer that time has been slowed to a standstill or stretched out to infinity. Like all accumulative repetition, it forces the viewer to become aware of subtleties, of minute variations that one would normally miss.

While introductory sections are extremely important for sensitizing and preparing the audience for the performance to come, encores have come to play a special role in Butō as well. In traditional theater there are no curtain calls--the closest approximation might be the "after-song" that the Nō chorus sings at the close of a performance to create the right mood for an ending, i.e., to return the audience to the jo level. Butō has borrowed the finale and curtain call of Western theater and dance, but true to form has significantly changed them: they are anything but simple bows. Unlike the Western theatrical tradition, where there is a distinct break between the ending of a performance

---

[59]For an evocative look at the influence of Zen on the Japanese avant garde of the late 1950's, see Haga Tōru, "The Japanese Point of View," in Avant-Garde Art in Japan (New York: Harry N. Abrams, Inc., 1962), unpaginated.

and the curtain calls, so that the actor leaves behind his performance persona and appears before us as "himself," in Butō curtain calls there is no diminution of tension, no real "post-performance" break out of character. They are instead completely choreographed, and have a distinct purpose and place within the structure of the work as a whole, usually taking the form of a short hand restatement and summation of the major choreographic ideas of the dance. Ichikawa Miyabi has mentioned in regards to the use of finales in Buto that, "when someone asked me what Butō's distinguishing characteristic was, I jokingly answered, 'Butō is created from the finale!'"[60] Ichikawa goes on to make a comparison between the thickly encrusted white makeup and the structure of time in Butō: "each layer of progress towards the finale paints on the face of Time another layer of white: the finale and curtain calls are the thick accumulation of Time's white makeup."[61]

Sankai Juku's curtain call at the end of the April 30 and 31, 1986 performance of Jōmon Shō was an effective example of the ways in which the curtain call acts to draw the entire dance into focus: standing at the far back with their bouquets cradled in their left arms, they all began swimming their right hands back and forth, flipping them up and down and around. As each dancer slowly drew his left leg back and sank downward to the floor, the hands rose in unison above the dancers' heads, still twisting frantically as though they had minds of their own, with the effect that, as the lights lowered and only their crouching silhouettes remained against the dark blue sky, it now looked as though the group were waving goodbye. The choreography of this curtain call touched again on the focal points of the entire dance: the precise articulation of separate parts of the body that resulted in the sense that a rational mind was not in control of the fragmented body, yet simultaneously a harmony of action between dancers that appeared to stem from a sharing of communal mind, a manifestation of a collective rather than individual will.

It is interesting to note that when Bando Tamasaburo, the Kabuki onnagata (female impersonator) who is something of a cult figure among young Japanese these days, performed at the Japan Society in 1984, his curtain call was equally as superb: one moment he was accepting bouquets from the audience, the next moment, with a single elegant undulation he had transformed himself into a graceful puddle of feminine humility on the stage floor.

---

[60]Ichikawa, "A Preface to Butō," p. 70.

[61]Ichikawa, "A Preface to Butō," p. 70.

There was no question of "breaking character": nothing could have so stunningly summed up the provocative eroticism of the onnagata's art.[62]

White Makeup

Ohno Kazuo has said that Butō dancers used white makeup in the early days to cover up the fact that they were still technically immature. Although this might be one explanation for the practice's origin, it doesn't really explain why white makeup has become one of Butō's most distinctive features. According to Ichikawa Miyabi, the first Butō dancers smeared chalk dissolved in glue on themselves to whiten their faces and bodies. Originally these bizarre encrustations were part of the attempt to turn the dancer into some alien "other"; Ichikawa says that their skin made him think of some kind of shellfish, perhaps a mollusk or barnacle.[63] As time went on, however, the dancers began using the same water-based makeup as Kabuki actors use, and from this point, the use of white makeup carried the additional resonance of its resemblance to Kabuki. Here again we have an example of how Butō uses the pastiche technique to incorporate onto itself, for its own purposes, techniques of traditional theater.

Within the Kabuki tradition, white face and body makeup has a number of meanings. Kabuki makeup is intended to both dramatically heighten the natural color of the skin, and to act as a surface on which an elaborate pattern of colored lines (kumadori) can be written. Kumadori signals to the viewer a whole range of meanings about the character being represented (i.e. whether the character is good, evil, god, mortal, ogre, man, woman, child, etc.) Thus, although Kabuki had left behind the idealized masks of Nō theater, the Kabuki face covered with white makeup and kumadori became a living mask that was simultaneously unique (as each person's face is unique) and yet symbolic of the collective ideal (inscribed by means of kumadori with the moral and religious codes of Japanese society).

In Butō kumadori is, of course, eliminated: there is no way to "read" the white makeup of the Butō dancer to learn his or her position in some wider moral context. At the same time, the white makeup and shaved head, and often the lack of costumes, strips the body of the usual identifying characteristics of the individual, i.e., any expressions of personal "taste," leaving only

---

[62]When performing in the West, even traditional Japanese performers will give in to Western custom and give curtain calls. However, as pointed out above, they retain their dramatic persona throughout.

[63]Ichikawa, "A Preface to Butō," p. 69.

the body's movement as the marker of difference. Each person has a particular way of moving, and that personal style is considered to be, "the most concrete, definite and pivotal aspect of the body, an absolute fundamental in the individual's body, immune to idealism or human will."[64]

In keeping with the origin of the practice, Butō dancers often layer the makeup extremely thickly and occasionally supplement it with white powder. This choice results in an interesting side effect: if layered thickly enough, during the performance it will continuously flake off in little wisps and eddies, so that the dancer, depending on his or her speed, seems to be either moving through or trailed by a fine white mist. The effect is rather subtle, especially since the dimness of the Butō stage normally only allows the audience to see the barest glimmer of white. Every once in a while, however, the effect is more pronounced, and although it could be interpreted in a number of ways, it seems to me when I see it that the skin of the dancer is literally crumbling away, disintegrating before my eyes. Marcia Siegel, on the other hand, describes the effect this way in her review of Muteki-sha: "reaching a pool of light, she turns, offers the flowers, weeps. A powdery dust rises from her as she moves. She could be smoldering."[65] It can also be used to more dramatic effect, as in this scene from Sankai Juku's Kinkan Shonen, which Arlene Croce describes as one of the "high moments of the evening":

> Dressed like a schoolboy in a cap and short pants, covered head to foot with white flour, mouthing silent syllables in cavern of silence, [Amagatsu Ushio] suddenly topples over backward, slamming the floor with such force that a white cloud rises from his clothing.[66]

However it is used, subtly or dramatically, this effect is one more element which helps to create the Butō vision of an unstable world in a state of constant flux, cyclically moving back and forth between the poles of disintegration and recreation.

Another reason that Butō dancers powder themselves with white is that its use helps make the dancer more highly visible, allowing the stage to be darkened far more that would otherwise be possible. It seems to me that

---

[64]Havens, Artist and Patron in Postwar Japan, p. 225.

[65]Marcia Siegel, "Flickering Stones," Village Voice (15 October 1985), p. 103.

[66]Arlene Croce, "Dancing in the Dark," New Yorker 60 (19 November 1985), p. 171.

this severely darkened stage which is the Butō trademark, characteristically returns to the original, premodern lighting practice of Japanese traditional theater. In premodern Nō and Kabuki, when there was no electric lighting so performances were lit by candles, little distinction was made between the lighting of the stage and the light on the audience, both being equally dim. Butō borrows traditional lighting practices in order to destroy the Western theatrical illusion of an "ideal" world up on the stage that is separate from the "real" world of the audience. It does so by contradicting Western lighting practice, which brightens the stage and leaves the audience in the dark in order to emphasize the distinction between the two. The undifferentiated darkness creates an atmosphere that imbues even the most grotesque images with an evocative, mysterious beauty. It was Tanizaki Jun'ichirō in In'ei Raisan (In Praise of Shadows) who first put forth the notion in 1933 that there was a traditional Japanese "aesthetic of darkness," that was being completely destroyed by the electric lights used in 20th century Kabuki and Nō: "a phosphorescent jewel gives off its glow and color in the dark and loses its beauty in the light of day."[67] Tanizaki links the darkness of the Nō stage with the world in which No was created: "the darkness in which Nō is shrouded and the beauty that emerges from it make a distinct world of shadows which today can be seen only on the stage; but in the past it could not have been far removed from daily life."[68] Butō's desire to bring back this aesthetic of darkness to theater can, in the same way, be linked to their desire to return to a premodern world where the Japanese found, "beauty not in the thing itself but in the patterns of shadows, the light and darkness that one thing against another creates."[69]

The Beshimi Kata

The Kabuki "mie," a kind of theatrical "freeze" that occurs at highly dramatic moments, intensifies the effect of kumadori makeup mentioned above, completely immobilizing the face and body in an expression and gesture that heightens the emotional power of the moment by its sheer extremity (the eyes bulge out and cross, the mouth stretches into an extraordinary grimace, the body seems to blow up to a superhuman size). While Butō

---

[67]Tanizaki Jun'ichirō, In Praise of Shadows, trans. Thomas J. Harper and Edward Seidensticker (New Haven, CT: Leete's Island Books, Inc., 1977), p. 30.

[68]Tanizaki, Shadows, p. 26.

[69]Tanizaki, Shadows, p. 30.

discards Kabuki's symbolic patterning of the face, in accordance with their strategy of stripping away specific meaning from particular gestures or techniques, it retains, albeit in a modified form, the mie.

Although, because of the Butō emphasis on metamorphosis--on the body constantly in motion, constantly changing--an actual freeze does not usually occur, there are often moments where a solo dancer stands alone and presents us with a virtuoso performance of the extremes of human expressivity. This is the kata called beshimi, a term the critic Iwabuchi Keisuke borrowed from the beshimi (grimace) mask in Nō.[70] Anna Kiselgoff, in her review of Muteki-sha's performance of Niwa at Asia Society, describes a clear example of the beshimi kata:

> Repeatedly the two performers transform their facial expressions into such extreme and different imagery during the seven episodes that they become virtually unrecognizable...Miss Nakajima, in particular, can tense up every fiber in her body, blow up each cheek or pucker each lip while turning her face into an eye-lolling "mask."[71]

Like Kabuki's "living mask" created through the use of kumadori and the mie, the continuously changing mask of beshimi in Butō aspires to the expression of the universal, but where the Kabuki mie transforms the character into a heroic figure of mythological proportions, the beshimi of Butō, which runs the gamut of all possible emotions, transforms each dancer into an "everyman" or "everywoman."

There were a number of ideas behind the development of beshimi: to begin with, it is an expression of pure metamorphosis, a grotesquery of a level that is impossible to pin down to any particular meaning and so transcends the limitations of dance that depends on the "imitation" of forms in the real world to convey its message. As Iwabuchi describes it:

> The body of the Butō dancer convulses endlessly. It is as though each fiber of the muscles has its own selfish autonomy and shudders violently as it pleases. It is not some kata that cries or is sad, it is the muscles themselves that are crying. The will does not move the muscles, the muscles themselves have their own will. The trembling of the limbs

---

[70]Iwabuchi, "The Paradigm of Butō," pp. 77.

[71]Anna Kiselgoff, "The Dance: Montreal Dance Festival," New York Times (23 September 1985), p. C27.

infects the spectator watching, too; this will of the muscles calls forth the penetrating power of the imagination so that mutual communication between audience and dancer occurs.[72]

The beshimi kata "infects" the audience on a pre-language, non-intellectual level through the release of emotions that have been so deeply repressed in contemporary society that when they break out into the open they will be able to negate our impulse to categorize with words such as "anger" or "love."

A second purpose for the beshimi is similar to that of the metamorphosis exercise and the use of violence: it is anti-individualistic, renouncing modernity's myth of the respect for the individual and purposefully aiming at the destruction of what Iwabuchi has called "the equation, face = individuality = identity."[73] By completely distorting the face out of all recognition the self is relieved of the tremendous pressure to be a distinct "personality" and is able to "fuse" back into a feeling of spiritual unity and tranquility with nature and with itself. By fragmenting the body--emphasizing the separation of the body from the control of the brain by random articulation of the individual parts--the goal of separating the body from the brain that has been filled with the institutional rubbish of modernity is achieved. By letting each body part convulse and spasm as it desires it establishes its freedom from the constraint of society which works its will through the mind of the dancer. I will return to this kata again in the last chapter, since Muteki-sha made extensive use of it in Niwa (The Garden).

Ganimata

Before turning to our analysis of Niwa (The Garden), I will deal with one last technique that has been borrowed from traditional theater and changed. This is the characteristic stance called ganimata, a name that might be translated as a "bowlegged crouch." Gōda Nario, who believes this to be the innovation that established Butō as a fully developed form, identifies its origination in a work by Hijikata of 1972, Shiki no Tame no 27 Ban (27 Nights for 4 Seasons). As he describes the technique, "the weight is hung on the outer sides of the two legs. When one 'floats' the inside of the legs upwards, the

---

[72]Iwabuchi, "The Paradigm of Butō," p. 75.

[73]Iwabuchi, "The Paradigm of Butō," p. 77.

knees will turn out of their own accord, and the entire frame of the body sinks down."[74]

There are a number of related reasons for the development of this distinctive stance in Butō. To begin with, there is ganimata's use in the metamorphosis exercise that plays such an important part in Butō training. When the dancers crouch down, a plane hovering 15 centimeters below the stage is created, from which the dancers are helped to experience the viewpoint of insects and animals.[75] "The act of crouching down, with arms hugging knees to make themselves as small as possible," Iwabuchi explains, "is a compression of the self's center, perhaps a reversion to the seed, egg, embryo, chrysalis, cocoon."[76]

The attempt to create a plane 15 centimeters below the stage might once again be seen as a borrowing from traditional dance techniques. Compare, for instance, the description of ganimata given above to the following description of the traditional technique of balancing weight in the hips, called hipparihai (oppositional tension) used in Nō and Kabuki:

> ...to block the hips while walking it is necessary to slightly bend the knees and, engaging the vertebral column, to use the trunk as a single unit, which then presses downward. In this way different tensions are created in the upper and lower parts of the body. These tensions oblige the body to find a new point of balance.[77]

Coincidental to this stress on a new center of gravity is the emphasis in Nō on the actor being solidly grounded, as the Kyōgen actor Nomura Mannojō makes clear:

> The actor must imagine that above him is suspended a ring of iron which is pulling him upwards and against which it is necessary to keep one's feet on the ground.[78]

It is easy to understand how this emphasis on "keeping one's feet on the ground" could have been seen by Butō dancers as the perfect way to counter ballet's expansive movement upward. Iwabuchi Keisuke emphasizes the

---

[74]Gōda, "On Ankoku Butō," p. 87

[75]Gōda, "On Ankoku Butō," p. 87.

[76]Iwabuchi, "The Paradigm of Butō," p. 76.

[77]Barba, "Theater Anthropology," p. 10.

[78]As quoted in Barba, "Theater Anthropology," p. 12.

contrast between Western modern dance and Butō, by comparing the style of the Butō groups Hoppō Butō-ha and Suzuran-tō with the German dance theorist Rudolf Laban's notion of the "kinesphere":

> In Laban's kinesphere, the basic stance is that of the human rising up, like a tower. In contrast to that, the basic position in the dance of Hoppō Butō-ha and Suzuran-tō is horizontal, level with, or below the earth's surface.[79]

There is in addition a symbolic resonance to the movement downward, as Tokyo Journal dance critic Marie Myerscough points out: "movements in Butō do not commence from the vertical and proceed up, presumably to the 'light,' but from a crouching position, out of which they spread down into 'darkness.'"[80]

One should note however, that although there are certainly strong similarities between ganimata and traditional theater's stress on balance in the hips, Hijikata was at pains to emphasize that ganimata had its source in the natural posture of the Japanese, particularly in the stance of farmers who had to constantly crouch down in their rice fields and who often had to carry extraordinarily heavy loads on their back. Although this stance, which reflects the rigor of premodern life, was disappearing rapidly because of urbanization and modernization, it lingered on in the more provincial parts of the country, particularly in the Tōhoku region where Hijikata was raised. From this perspective, ganimata could be seen as a "natural" stance for the Japanese body, and in fact its genesis has been located by Gōda Nario in "Hijikata's skillful questioning of his own body" through which "he revealed to us its birthplace and formation; that is, he returned to the landscape of Akita."[81] The emphasis on ganimata as a natural posture ties in with Hijikata's belief that the body is a repository for unconscious collective memory and that by recreating (or reliving) certain postures those memories will be reactivated in the viewer as well as the dancer, by means of a direct preverbal channel of communal identity.

---

[79]Iwabuchi, "The Paradigm of Butō," p. 76. In Laban's book, Choreutics, the term kinesphere is defined as "the sphere around the body whose periphery can be reached by easily extended limbs...." Rudolf Laban, Choreutics (London: MacDonald and Evans, 1966), p. 10.

[80]Myerscough, "Butō," p. 8.

[81]Gōda, "On Ankoku Butō," p. 85.

The seeming contradiction between Butō's disavowal of technique, and their adoption of kata like ganimata is often played out in comments like the following, in which Amagatsu Ushio discusses an exercise that involves the ganimata stance that Sankai Juku uses in training: "it teaches the students to work against tension and toward a natural body...It is getting to certain natural states rather than learning some technique or form."[82] The question of how "natural" Butō training is becomes most evident when watching Sankai Juku: one is struck again and again by the dancers' virtuoso performance of feats only the most highly trained (and thus unnatural) of bodies could perform. However, whatever the final decision on whether to call forms like ganimata and beshimi "techniques" or not, Hijikata made it very clear what he believed their ultimate goal was to be:

> Butō plays with time; it also plays with perspective, if we humans learn to see things from the perspective of an animal,insect, even inanimate objects. That road trodden every day is alive...we should value everything.[83]

---

[82]Ushio Amagatsu as quoted in Jennifer Dunning, "Sankai Juku at City Center," New York Times (2 November 1984).

[83]Myerscough, "Butō," p. 8.

Chapter Three

ANALYSIS OF NIWA (THE GARDEN)

Muteki-sha is a second generation Butō group directed and choreographed by Nakajima Natsu. Nakajima was born in 1943 on the island of Sakhalin, about 20 miles off the coast of Hokkaido (the northernmost island of Japan). After World War II when the island was taken by Russia, all the Japanese were evacuated by sea and forced to leave their homes and most of their possessions behind. The trauma of that event has been captured for Nakajima in the sound of the ship's foghorn (the muteki), which "still resonates in her memory and her work."[1] She began taking dance classes in 1955, studying ballet and modern dance in Tokyo until 1962, when she saw her first performance of Ankoku Butō. She was deeply impressed by the performance, seeing in it an alternative to Western dance forms and principles and immediately began studying with Hijikata Tatsumi and Ohno Kazuo. "In some ways," Nakajima has said, "I feel that I was the first real student of Hijikata and Ohno. Before me there was Ishii (Mitsutaka) and Kasai (Akira), but they were more like colleagues than students."[2] That year (1962-63) a group of dancers was meeting on the weekends in Hijikata's studio. According to Nakajima, "Ohno was mostly teaching improvization; Hijikata gave us a list of books to read during the week. We'd gather together on Friday and work non-stop--whenever we weren't dancing, we were discussing books. It was kind of crazy, but I was only nineteen at the time, so it was very exciting for me."[3]

---

[1]Niwa (The Garden), program notes for performance at The Asia Society, New York City, September 27 and 28, 1985.

[2]Nakajima Natsu, interview with the author, 5 February 1988.

[3]Nakajima, interview.

55

At some point that year Hijikata and Ohno went their separate ways, and from then on Hijikata refused to teach improvization. Instead, he became more interested in developing a new formal vocabulary for dance, a new range of techniques more suitable for the Japanese body. Nakajima felt that she had to choose between Ohno and Hijikata, and although she kept in close contact with Ohno, she elected to study with Hijikata. In 1969 she left his studio to form her own company, which she named after the foghorn whose sound expressed for her the very personal psychological trauma caused by the wider play of super-power politics.

Niwa (The Garden), a two act performance lasting about 100 minutes, was presented for the first time in Tokyo in 1982. It had its North American premiere at the Montreal Dance Festival on September 18 and 19, 1985, and was presented for the first time in the United States at The Asia Society in New York City on September 27 and 28. In the following discussion the program is briefly outlined, a few generalized comments are made on the structure and theme, and then the entire piece is analyzed section by section to show how Nakajima's work fits into the Butō aesthetic as described in the previous pages. I only saw Niwa once in live performance; nevertheless because I found this piece one of the most compelling, as well as exemplary, of the Butō performances I have seen, I have chosen to work with it. As it happens, I was able to clear up a number of uncertainties by viewing a video made of the performance as well as by interviewing Nakajima herself.

The program was divided up into seven sections as follows:[4]

Nanakusa. Dance of seven autumn flowers, recollections of childhood. Dry flowers rustle with sadness or pleasure. Muttering lips recall the spring garden, calling and playing with cherry blossoms falling in the wind. (Nakajima)

The Infant as a baby evacuated from Sakhalin, the world is viewed from a boat as a hell, chaos and shouting, exhaustion and the defeat of soldiers. (Maezawa)

The Dream of the girl is a sweet dream, the dream of the child becomes the nightmare of the adult, return to the girl in the forest, shimmering light. (Nakajima and Maezawa)

---

[4]The following descriptions are taken from Niwa (The Garden) program notes.

Izumeko. The baby lives within the tiny world of the cradle --eating, sleeping, playing--tiny, but with a primitive energy. (Maezawa)

Masks and Black Hair. Old age masks recall her mature womanhood--her black hair and the memories of love. (Nakajima)

Ghost. Regret for lost days reflected in the face--loss of power, weakness of muscle, loss of features and all human character. (Nakajima)

Kannon. World of innocence, stillness--fluent energy of eternity. (Nakajima)

Another dancer, Maezawa Yuriko, joined Nakajima in this program. As indicated in the program given above, in the first half the two dancers alternated section by section. The white makeup, which in Butō acts to mask particular individuality, was here used to good effect: it allowed the two dancers to play one character, the single role of Nakajima as child, young girl, old woman, ghost, and Buddha. In only one scene were the two dancers on stage together; the section in "The Dream" where they were transformed into two insects in a garden. Otherwise there were never any "duets" (although occasionally one was coming on stage as the other was leaving). Since the two dancers could be seen as two aspects, two sides of the one woman's character,[5] the overall effect was of an evening length solo.

In the program notes, Nakajima describes the piece this way:

Niwa is a forgotten garden, very small and very Japanese, this is the garden of my memory, my childhood...I created this work to see my own life, placing myself as a woman, sitting in the garden, looking at it grow old and fade away.[6]

---

[5]According to her Village Voice review, Marcia Siegel perceived it that way: "They seem to be two aspects of the woman: Natsu Nakajima, the choreographer, is the one who suffers and changes, Yuriko Maesawa (sic) is more playful and demonic.." Siegel, "Flickering Stones," p. 103. Although it seems like an obvious response to the strategy of using two dancers to play one character, I was unable to make such a clear distinction in personality between the two dancers.

[6]Niwa (The Garden), program notes.

The darkened stage thus represented the darkened inner space of the mind, with the various tableaux presented as if seen through memory's distorting mirror. And like memory, while the sections could be intellectually reordered to form a chronological sequence (beginning with pre-birth and ending with enlightenment), the actual ordering was not so straight-forward: 1) young woman offering flowers, 2) infant, 3) young girl in garden, 4) infant, 5) old woman, 6) ghost reliving the woman's prime, 7) Kannon. In performance the individual images flowed together as though called up by a process of association, a process set off by the accident of metaphoric similarity or metynomic congruence, rather than by the linear narrative chronology of cause and effect.

The overall structure of time in the piece (that is, the cyclical movement from birth to rebirth), combined with the non-linear quality of the linkage of imagery, accords well with the model of metempsychosis that I discussed in the previous chapter. The structure of the dance program has two interconnecting sets of cycles: one is the overarching metempsychosic cycle, which begins with a Shinto ritual, moves through life, and ends with Buddhist enlightenment. This movement also happens to parallel the pattern of ritual in Japanese religious life: ceremonies that have to do with life, such as birth and marriage, are usually Shinto, while those that have to do with death tend to be Buddhist. The second set is the smaller cycles of jo-ha-kyū rhythm and pacing, in which moments of peace and tranquility give way to dances that illustrate the pain and suffering of existence, climaxing in solo dances in front of the spotlight that end abruptly in a crescendo of noise and excitement, before cycling back to another moment of peace, that is however, at a higher level of tension than before.

Whereas Amagatsu Ushio's Sankai Juku uses the metempsychosic mode to present us with an archetypal vision of the **collective** unconscious, particularly in his visions of prehistory, Nakajima follows in Ohno Kazuo's footsteps in her attempt to show us how that mode can be used to reveal the inner workings of the subconscious level of the **individual** psyche. The opening scene of Niwa can be seen as a kind of pre-birth God time; there is the trauma of childhood, the dream of a young girl, the memories of old age, the experience of death and the ghost's longing for the past, and finally, rebirth as Buddha.

And while Sankai Juku literalizes Zen's "fall of self" in their signature piece from Jōmon Shō (Homage to Prehistory), in which four of the dancers, nearly naked, hang suspended head-first from the proscenium and are slowly lowered to the stage, in Niwa, a more political dimension is added. The dance as a whole points toward the negativity attached to the position of the individual self--traumatized psychologically as a child by powers it cannot control, alienated and isolated as an adult and as an old woman, in the end swept away by catastrophic change--in order to contrast it with scenes of communal bliss that illustrated the ecstatic joy to be had when one loses one's sense of individual self in the great cosmic unconsciousness, what art historian Haga Tōru has called, "the bottomless and formless (or, rather, preformed) I."[7]

Turning now to the analysis of Niwa: after a prefatory section in which one of Astor Piazola's lively modern tangos is played as slides of autumn scenery are projected, the dance itself opens in absolute darkness to strongly rhythmic electronic music. For the space of a minute or so, one cannot make out anything at all, even the stage. Slowly one begins to see a vague form, a glimmer at the far back, at stage-left. Soon it becomes apparent that there is a dancer there, making her way forward by imperceptible inches. It is significant that the dance begins here, as this space is considered the most "jo" of the jo area of the stage, and thus is the most appropriate place to begin a dance as agonizingly slow as this one. In fact, this opening is very much in line with what the jo aesthetic calls for in an opening dance, that is, it puts the audience into an attentive and felicitous mood. There is a very strong tension between the driving beat of the repetitive electronic music and the unbelievably slow pace of her movement. As in other Butō opening sequences, this minimal, repetitive movement combined with trance-inducing music, creates a mystical feeling of great depth, as well as a heightened feeling of awareness. In fact, Marcia Siegel's review provides us with a good example of how one begins to read all kinds of emotional changes into the minutest variation in gesture: "without changing her expression at all, [Nakajima] seems to be turning away, hesitating, recoiling, submitting, but never ceasing her advance."[8]

This use of tension fits perfectly into the definition of jo put forth recently by Eugenio Barba: "The first phrase is determined by the opposition between a force which tends to increase and another which tends to hold back (jo = withhold)."[9] In addition to the powerful outer tension between the dancer's movement and the music, there is also a great divided tension within her body: her upper torso is tilted far back, yet her arms stretch forward and

---

[7]Haga, "Japanese Point of View," unpaginated.

[8]Siegel, "Flickering Stones," p. 103.

[9]Barba, "Theater Anthropology," p. 22. I should note however, that although this definition fits the opening of Niwa extremely well, I have been unable to verify this definition of jo as "to withhold" in any source on Nō.

upwards, in order to hold out a bundle of dried flowers (the nanakusa or "seven grasses"). She seems to be offering up the flowers to someone or something (to us? to an unseen god?), and this gesture emphasizes the dialectical tension between her slow approach towards us and this stretching backward arch, so that she appears to be gripped by an invisible power which mercilessly pulls her forward against her will.

In the first half of a typical Nō play a local woman or man appears who presents an offering to the gods. In the course of the play the woman turns out to be possessed by a ghost tormented by an attachment to the past, who seeks Buddhist salvation. The climax of the play comes when the ghost is released from its attachment through the telling of his or her story and thus receives enlightenment.[10] In "Nanakusa," the opening scene of Niwa, we seem to be in the presence of exactly the same kind of young woman that opens a Nō play; a woman making an offering to the gods. Or perhaps, going back to the original basis for Nō, she is a shamanistic miko caught up in the ritual trance that is her art. In addition, the bundle of dried flowers and grasses strongly suggest that we are witnessing some kind of harvest ritual. This use of harvest/agricultural metaphors (repeated later on in the portrayal of a farm woman) corresponds with Butō's attempt to go back to the spiritual roots of dance/drama in Japan, since, as Komparu Kunio points out:

> sacred agricultural festivals formed the basis for nearly all
> the entertainment arts in Japan, and in them we see clearly
> a tendency toward cycles and assimilation with nature that
> might even be called the foundation of Japanese culture,
> created by a farming people.[11]

Returning to our analysis of the dance: at long last, after what has seemed like an infinite amount of time, but has probably been less than 15 minutes, Nakajima reaches the moment of ha (or "break"): suddenly liberated from the force of jo she freely enters a pool of bright light, center

---

[10]Of course there are a number of other possible narrative structures for a Nō play, but the one given above is seen as the most typical. This model strongly suggests Nō's original basis in the ritual performance of an exorcism, in which a possessed miko, or shamaness, becomes a mouthpiece for a tormented ghost who has sought attention for her or his case by possessing someone. For a comprehensive treatment of shamanistic practices in Japan, see Carmen Blacker, The Catalpa Bow (London: George Allen and Unwin, 1986).

[11]Komparu, The Noh Theater, p. 4.

stage. Having made it to the central, __ha__ part of the stage, she turns to us, raising her flowers higher, and we can see the tears of release pouring down her cheeks. Here again I was struck by a resemblance to Nō, particularly in the emphasis on her arrival as being some kind of epiphany; I suddenly recalled the famous definition by the French poet and dramatist, Paul Claudel: "Le Drame, c'est quelqueque chose qui arrivé, le Nō, c'est quelquun qui arrivé" (In drama, something happens, in Nō, someone arrives).[12]

The lights drop and the __ha__ level continues in the next section, "The Infant," which begins as the second dancer, Maezawa, comes on stage from the rear. This is a reenactment of Nakajima's traumatic evacuation from Sakhalin as a child after World War II. Everything emphasizes the helplessness of the child in the face of super-power politics, whose terrifying force is represented both as a hurricane wind that sends the child tottering from one end of the stage to the other, and as a barrage of chaotic noise that assaults us at top volume. The section reaches its climax as she comes all the way downstage to squat in front of the full force of a spotlight angled upwards.

Here the dancer is fulfilling the requirements for __kyū__ spatially (all the way downstage, right up against the audience) and aurally (we hear a tape loop of Wagner which keeps cutting off just at the melodic climax, frustrating us over and over again). Her dance also fulfills those requirements visually (in Nō a __kyū__ piece should be an "exuberant spectacle of vigorous gestures, rapid dancing and strenuous movements that fill the audience with wonder"[13]) as Maezawa goes into the __beshimi__ __kata__, the Butō visual tour-de-force of expression.

This particular __beshimi__ is a marvelous example of the Butō technique in which the body acts as a container of fluid whose constant flow keeps internal and external pressure in precarious balance. At first Maezawa reacts to the noise, the fury of the music, as though it were not external to her but rather, the external expression of what is happening **inside** her. This results in a sense that devastation is welling up like water, a fluid psychological energy

---

[12]In the French there is a play on "arrivé," which can mean both "to arrive" and "to happen."

[13]Komparu, The Noh Theater, p. 26. Nō plays have themselves been divided into categories according to __jo-ha-kyū__; I should note that albeit quite apt here, the description quoted above is of a __kyū__ dance from a play that is itself categorized as __kyū__ (a fifth category, or "demon" play). The dance described is therefore much more powerful than a __kyū__ dance in a __jo__ play (first category, or "god" play) would be.

that thrusts outwards through her puffed cheeks and bulging eyes, threatening to burst at any moment. Then there is a reversal; suddenly one senses that she is deep **under** water, and all her gestures seem to indicate that she is holding her breath, struggling to get to the surface as though she were trapped in an oppressive, suffocating nightmare. Paradoxically, Maezawa's performance is an exhibition of almost perfect control over movements that on the surface seem to epitomize a utter lack of control over the ways in which psychological pressures of internal anxiety and external oppression affect the body.

During the beshimi sections of Niwa (which repeated at regular intervals throughout the dance) a very effective form of lighting was used to dramatize the strange contortions of the dancer: a single spotlight was angled upwards from below, less than a foot from the dancer's face as she crouched down. Once again this seems to be an example of a technique borrowed from traditional performance practice, in this case from Edo period Kabuki. In the Edo period there was, of course, no electric lighting and when an actor was going to do a mie, a kōken (stage assistant) would hold up a candle right under his face, so that the flickering light from below lent greater dramatic ferocity, even a supernatural aura to the pose. In Niwa too, the single spotlight used in a completely darkened stage adds a much heightened dramatic force to the "mie-in-motion" that is beshimi.

After this climax, the third section, "The Dream," brings us back down to the jo level of an idyllic garden scene. It opens with a young girl in a long dress, a scarf knotted around her throat. She crouches down, fluttering her fingers in gentle waves. When the second dancer enters, they seem to metamorphose into insects. Long steel springs act as their antennae, keeping them constantly in touch with their surroundings, which the dappled lighting indicates is a garden (the set is minimal). Occasionally the springs also act as balancing poles that literally keep the dancers' bodies in balance as they explore an imaginary natural world. The insects' intimate relationship with nature and with each other is emphasized by the fact that this is the only time the two dancers are on stage together. The contrast with the chaos of the preceding scene could not be more explicit: only in the natural world is communion (or even connection) to other living beings possible.

The lights go down and when they come up again a young woman stands alone downstage right, her head bowed to the left. The music, heavy and ominous, seems to oppress the woman as she struggles to lift up her head. She looks helpless, overwhelmed. The idyllic garden scene has been left far behind as "The Dream" reaches its climax in another beshimi. In the first act we have thus cycled twice through the pacing of jo-ha-kyū. The kyū climax in the spotlight, which occurred at least one more time in the second half of the program,[14] emphasized the internal structure of jo-ha-kyū repetition by its regular alternation with the meditative sections of "Nanakusa," "The Dream, and "Kannon."

As part 2, "Izumeko" (literally, "basket baby"[15]), opens we are again plunged into total darkness. Soon however, we can make out a large, rounded object, placed downstage stage-right, which seems to be a simple woven basket. As the lights come up a bit, we can see that someone is hunched inside it. Suddenly, bright eyes appear over the rim, followed cautiously by the rest of the figure, dressed in a scarlet kimono. In this transitional section Maezawa could be either a child who is afraid of the dark, or a figure of evil checking to make sure that no one is around before it begins its witchery. The creature-- whether child or woman--clambers stealthily out of her basket/cradle, holding up a lantern to peer out into the dark, while the murmur of chanting and the high-pitched sound of a shakahachi flute begins.

Maezawa then starts on a series of wide loops around the stage, her knees bent, her arms spread wide, her fingers crooked in classic witch style. It was at this point that one could see most clearly the German Expressionist influence of Mary Wigman. As it happens, I saw the film fragment of Wigman's Witch Dance the week before I saw Muteki-sha's performance, and I could not help being struck by certain similarities. Wigman describing the origin of Witch Dance in her book of essays, The Language of Dance, might very well have been describing the dancer in "Izumeko": "when one night, I returned to my room utterly agitated, I looked into the mirror by chance. What it reflected was the image of one possessed, wild, dissolute, repelling and fascinating...there she was--the witch--the earth-bound creature with her unrestrained, naked instincts, with her insatiable lust for life, beast and

---

[14]This is one place my notes break down for the second half. I know that in the second act there was a climactic beshimi section in which both Maezawa and Nakajima performed, down front on opposite sides of the stage, but I have been unable to discern from my notes exactly where in the performance this occurred, and so I have been forced to leave it out of my analysis.

[15]In Japanese farming communities during the busy harvest season no one could be spared to look after the small children, so they were often tied into a basket called an izume and left by the side of the field. Hijikata claimed that when he was a child he was one of these "basket babies," and that the experience of being bound and unable to move for long periods of time had left an indelible mark on his body.

woman at the same time."[16] The continuous movement from the gloom of upstage to the relative brightness of downstage and back furthers the resemblance to Wigman, who felt that "through the play of question and answer between a remote background plunged in twilight and glaring foreground action" the Witch Dance's true character could be found.[17]

At the beginning of "Izumeko," Maezawa seems to simultaneously control, and to be controlled by, the forces that she has called up. However, as the dance progresses, there is the sound of a great wind rising, and with arms spread wide (incidentally revealing the gorgeousness of the lining of her kimono) the dancer gives herself up to the force of the wind, blowing backwards around the stage like a brightly colored kite. During one of these wide loops, Maezawa runs briefly offstage right, and Nakajima comes back on with the kimono; a trick to make the casual observer believe it is the same woman. From Nakajima's entrance onstage, however, the woman's movement changes: she seems to gradually grow more and more feeble, so that every movement forward, taking place in small, painful increments and accompanied by the shaking of old age, begins to look extraordinarily difficult. As "Izumeko" ends, Nakajima turns from downstage and bends to pick up a bundle, simultaneously taking on what until recently has been the characteristic stance of old people in rural Japan, bent over practically double at the waist from a lifetime of carrying heavy loads. As we watch, she sheds the bright red kimono, and at the far back of the stage (spatially signalling a cyclical return once again to the peace and quiet of a jo phase) she dons a grey mask and kerchief, so that when she turns to face us, she has taken on the persona of an extremely old farm woman.

The use of the mask here seems significant on a number of levels. First, it is overtly marked by its direct contradiction of the usual Butō makeup, which emphasizes the humanity of the character portrayed:

> The white face of the Geisha represents a being transfixed, but the whitened face of the Butō dancer is the moving face

---

[16]Mary Wigman, The Language of Dance, trans. Walter Sorell (Middletown, CT: Wesleyan University Press, 1966) pp. 40-41. I was not the only one to note this resemblance; Marcia Siegel also pointed it out in her review: "I imagined it all as the lost sections of Mary Wigman's Witch Dance." Siegel, "Flickering Stones, p. 103. Coincidentally, Ohno Kazuo is presently at work on a dance based on Witch Dance, that he plans to present next year.

[17]Wigman, Language of Dance, p. 42.

of humanity, actually in touch with innocence, wonder, fear, and mortality.[18]

In Niwa we are instead presented with a very different face, a mask face colored grey, emptied of expression. It makes an interesting comparison to the calm, neutral type of Nō mask, called ko-omote (the young woman mask), which has little expression of its own, but instead invites us to project our own feelings onto it. The vacant, haggard look of the mask in Niwa reflects the heavy oppression of the farming woman's life, and reveals by its very inexpressiveness the ways in which society acts on individuals to cut off and control their access to their natural instincts, to their natural sources of emotional expression.

A second reason for choosing to use a mask might be that the disruption of gaze caused by the mask (we cannot see the dancer's living eyes, and the dancer's sight is itself disrupted), is linked to both a loss of humanity (eye contact being one of the most fundamental of human gestures) and to a loss of contact with the phenomenal world. In Japan, old age is traditionally supposed to bring a progressive detachment from material things. This detachment is both actively sought after (by "taking the tonsure," i.e. shaving one's head and becoming a Buddhist monk), and passively suffered (the loss of sight, hearing etc., that comes naturally with old age). The idea is that this Buddhist renunciation of worldly life prepares one for death and the enlightenment that comes only to those who have freed themselves from the delusion of worldly attachments.

As "Masks and Black Hair" continues, the woman kneels quietly at the rear of the stage. She hits her neck with the palm of her hand once or twice (a sign that is culturally defined in Japan to mean the stiff neck of old age), taps her knees in time to the music for a bit, and then slowly begins to mime such daily activities as eating soba noodles, playing the Japanese lute, pouring tea, and sewing. She then comes forward to where she left the red kimono. She picks it up and cradles it, slips her hands into its sleeves, and holding them up to her face, finally pulls it over her head. When she reemerges out from under the robe, she has exchanged the grey mask for a red one. Once again the stage business reminded me of a traditional technique from Nō. Here the sudden emergence of the red mask from under the kimono bore a remarkable

---

[18]Lizzie Slater as cited in David Wilk, "Profound Perplexing Sankai Juku," The Christian Science Monitor (8 November 1984). Wilk here quotes from Slater's essay in the program for a Sankai Juku performance at the Boston Opera House, Fall 1984.

resemblance to the scene in the Nō play Aoi no Ue, where a woman possessed by jealousy is transformed into a demoness. In the Nō play, the woman enters with a kimono pulled over her head, and after much suspense, at last lifts the kimono to reveal a horrifying demon mask, tinted red. In Nō a mask tinted red often signifies the wearer is a ghost with supernatural power or is possessed by demonic forces. A Japanese ghost differs somewhat from the Western conception of a ghost, and the ghost that characteristically appears in Nō plays has a lot in common with the ghost that appears in Niwa, as can be seen from the following description of a Nō ghost by Kunio Komparu:

> a human being who has departed from this world but maintains some kind of attachment becomes a ghost, and at the moment of death such a person loses the future and is fixed into an eternal present. The only time allowed is the past. Thus, the ghost always appears as the figure it was in life and reminisces about the single experience of profound memory that entraps it within the web of delusion.[19]

On the edge of death, the woman in Niwa was remembering the prosaic, ordinary activities of her lifetime on a farm. Now, she has become a goryō, the Japanese ghost who is doomed to be an ageless wanderer, a perpetual refugee driven from place to place with no rest in sight. The reenactment in death of Nakajima's experience in life of being a political refugee brings the section to yet another kyū climax, as a storm of sound repeats and amplifies the chaos of the Sakhalin section. The last image we see is of the woman/ghost frantically running back and forth across the stage with one arm above her head as though to ward off approaching catastrophe. Grabbing up her bundle, she finally escapes from the stage as the music/noise reaches the peak of its crescendo.

When the woman returns to the stage, the mask is gone. Now, we seem to be watching her reenact a **positive** memory of her youth. As popular music begins to play (a kitschy, romantic mixture of lieder music, dance hall, accordion, and tango) the woman appears to become a singer or a dancer in a nightclub. Eyes closed, arm curved above her head as though she were about to plunge into a flamenco dance, she looks as though she were drowning in ecstacy as she remembers her long lost beauty. At this moment in particular one can see traces of the influence of Ohno Kazuo: the resemblance to portions of Ohno's Admiring La Argentina were truly striking.

---

[19]Komparu, The Noh Theater, p. 86. This description is of course not necessarily true of all Nō plays, but only for those in which a ghost appears.

In the classic Nō manner, the simple act of retelling the memory through dance allows the dancer's release from her attachment and as the Bailero from Songs of the Auvergne comes on, the woman achieves enlightenment. In the last section of the dance, her final transformation into the Bodhisattva Kannon transforms her into a living statue that glows with golden light as she slowly assumes iconic poses from the statuary of all the major religions, including Christian, Buddhist and Hindu. The dance has returned once again to the jo phase, to a "world of innocence, stillness--fluent energy of eternity."[20]

As a final note, I'd like to point to at least one way that Butō has been influenced by Japanese traditions other than performance. Although I have suggested above some of the similarities between the structure of Niwa and the premodern religious structure of the Japanese life, in closing one might note that it is not only in the structure of Butō pieces that the influence of Buddhism is found. The Butō use of beshimi and other metamorphosis-based improvisation techniques aimed at bringing the body into mystical union with nature can be seen as grounded in Zen Buddhism as well. Following in a long tradition of essentially irrational art, these improvisations might be compared to Zen kōans, the improvisatory, poetic-symbolic paradoxes that the art historian Haga Tōru has described as, "discharges of an intense energy that should pierce at once and suddenly illumine the darkness of our confused minds."[21] The darkness of the soul in Ankoku Butō, which rejects our analytical interpretations, can be seen as a necessary step towards enlightenment, that is, the necessary "fall of self" into darkness that proceeds the light of mystical oneness with nature:

> At the end of the arduous and assiduous path of negation...the very foundation of self will be shattered...disclosing within us an abyss in which will be diffused, pure and innocent, the light that is Buddha. Such is the crucial experience of 'the fall of the self'...which led St. John of the Cross beyond illuminations and ecstasies to the 'dark night of the soul' and to 'the sonorous solitude.'[22]

Ankoku Butō, "dark soul dance" or "the dance of utter darkness," has its philosophical basis in this "dark night of the soul" which allows us to wrench

---

[20]Niwa (The Garden), program notes.

[21]Haga, "Japanese Point of View," unpaginated.

[22]Haga, "Japanese Point of View," unpaginated.

free "from the restricting, additive, static humanistic vision of the world."[23] In this sense, the very attempt to analyze Butō in the manner undertaken in this essay may be seen as essentially contradictory to its spirit, since such an analysis reduces the works' possible meanings by employing the explanatory apparatus of rational thought. Although most audiences need some background for Butō to seem anything more than a new wave of spectacularly visual expressionist theater, one should always keep in mind that this attachment to critical analysis is, from the perspective of the Butō dancer within the Japanese artistic tradition, a delusion. By way of conclusion, it seems apt to paraphrase a description taken from an essay by Haga Tōru on Japanese avant-garde art, as an illustration of how the Butō dancer in the last section of Niwa would herself wish to be seen: as a figure advancing inexorably toward enlightenment, exorcising the ghosts of interpretations, those demons who blind us to the true reality, while it simultaneously causes the collapse of that scaffolding of concepts which clutter up our meager intellect, in order to restore us, as it were, to ourselves, to our original selves.[24]

---

[23]Haga, "Japanese Point of View," unpaginated.

[24]Haga, "Japanese Point of View," unpaginated.

Appendix A

"A Preface to Butō"

by

Ichikawa Miyabi

If postmodernism's escape from the modern era lies in the ordeal of somehow getting **beyond** modernism, Butō, which is based on an Asian philosophy of the unity of the body and the soul, is a current flowing **back** towards the premodern era. Butō was born more than 20 years ago, a bit earlier than Western postmodern dance. A long time has passed since then.[1]

The 1980 appearance of Ohno Kazuo and Sankai Juku at the Nancy Dance Festival in France was the turning point that signalled Butō's assumption of a leading role in the international dance scene. Although Ashikawa Yōko and the group Butō-ha Sebi had given sporadic performances in Europe before then, after 1980 Butō's popularity swelled so rapidly that, astonishingly enough, they sold out the Paris Opera House. At the 1982 Avignon Festival, Ohno Kazuo appeared along with Dai Rakuda-kan, and in 1983 Hijikata Tatsumi's group participated in the "Six Country Festival" in Europe.

Although the look of Butō has a number of unique features, the strangely transfigured appearance of the body is probably the most characteristic. Butō dancers wear white makeup. At first, the dancers smeared themselves with white chalk dissolved in glue, so that their skin had a bizarre roughness like that of a shellfish. These days, however, they simply mix white makeup with water and paint themselves, so their white skin seems no different from that of a Kabuki actor. Why is it that this white makeup has become such a characteristic feature of Butō?

According to Ohno Kazuo, in the early years the dancers relied on white makeup to cover up the fact that their technique was still undeveloped.

---

[1]This translation is from Ichikawa Miyabi, " 'Butō' Josetsu," in Butō: Nikutai no Suriarisutotachi (Butō: Surrealists of the Flesh), ed. Hanaga Mitsutoshi (Tokyo: Gendai Shokan, 1983), unpaginated.

As far as this goes, if it is true then Butō dancers are left without a leg to stand on. It might be alright for someone like Ohno, whose technique is beyond question, to say something like this, but it renders everyone else "immature." Actually, though, Ohno's opinion on this point is probably, on some level, on target. On the other hand, even if their technique **was** insufficient, the conceptual element of Butō was so striking that it compensated for any immaturity.

The use of white makeup was probably encouraged by two of Butō's major components: the repression of seething desire and the will to metamorphosis which would transform the body into something grotesque. In the early 1960's Hijikata was given to explosive exclamations of "No!" and "It's all wrong!". He was constantly worrying about the meaning of modern dance (buyō); even as he rejected it, he must have felt his own ego surfacing. However, Butō dancers choose to repress their desires rather than express them. Rather than emotion, it is form that is primary. From out of this experience of wrestling with will and desire, Hijikata finally chose forms that had been distorted, such as the white makeup and the eyes that roll up into the sockets. When someone once asked me what Butō's distinguishing characteristic was, I jokingly answered, "Butō is created from the finale!" It seems to me now that that reply is more profound than I originally thought. Working from the point of view of the structure of time in Butō, each layer of progress towards the finale paints on the face of Time another layer of white; the finale and curtain calls are thus the thick accumulation of Time's white makeup. Within Hijikata there was an inclination for stoicism and a dandyism that would not openly reveal sexual desire.

Ohno Kazuo's female impersonation of Divine, Hijikata Tatsumi's Nikutai no Hanran (Revolt of the Flesh) and Anma (The Blind Masseur), Ashikawa Yōko's Ebisu-ya Ocho (Ocho of Ebisu House), Kasai Akira's various dazzling transformations, Dai Rakuda-kan's festive, carefree chaos, the Butō group Ariadne's spread-leg perversities: each and every one is based in the metamorphosis of the body. One can see their desire to transfigure the body expressed not only in the use of white makeup, but in shaving their heads as well. No matter what form it takes, the fundamental attitude of Butō is the negation of the body itself through powerful metamorphosis.

If we look at Butō in the context of the current attempt to transcend modernism, we can see that our modern institutions infiltrate every nook and cranny of people's bodies. Having been thoroughly violated by this institutionalizing process, people must turn on their own bodies a violent hatred in order to be able to stand on their feet again. Hijikata's work from the early 1960's reveals a strong interest in making dances that were violent, in dealing with the theme of homosexuality, and in severely tormenting the body, even going so far as to attempt to dismember it. Men were forced to become women, the dancers had to become all sorts of imaginary beasts and monsters. This aggression directed towards the body was, naturally enough, unacceptable by commonly shared moral standards, and for long years Butō was treated as an underground performance art.

The use of metamorphosis in Butō appears as part of a process of restoring to the self "the body that has been robbed," and as such its purpose differs from the Baroque use of metamorphosis. Utilizing court ballet tricks, the structure of the spectacle is based on the dual personality, or constant metamorphosis, of various characters, so that eventually, as it becomes impossible to tell one person from another, the individual subject disappears altogether. Lurking behind all this is a principle which looks suspiciously like the Baroque idea that energy is indestructible, but I believe Butō's use of metamorphosis has a more ethical basis. The more groups like Dai Rakuda-kan and Dance Love Machine stress Rabelaisian phantasmagoria, the more distinctly their desire to fragment the self stands out.

In Europe quite a few people in the audience were moved to tears. This was probably because they saw what to them must have seemed impossible: the will attempting to negate the world by fracturing the body that is seen as its microcosm, torturing it and forcing it to submit to disfiguring transformations. This was not some scene of premodern Japan or exorcism. The audience was inspired by the complex way in which these dancers, who they could see experienced the contemporary world just as they did, were addressing the question of how we will live through these last few dying moments of the modern era.

Appendix B

"The Paradigm of Butō"

by

Iwabuchi Keisuke

It is said that dance has two origins. One theory explains dance as a biological instinct. Our arms, left and right, are symmetrical to each other, and our hearts beat out a regular rhythm. Space exclusively possessed by a single human being is created when a person stands with legs spread out and both arms outstretched and waving. Rudolf Von Laban (German, 1894-1958), who is called the father of modern dance, defined dance as "the spatial art" and he attached the name "kinesphere"[2] to the spherical space in which the dancer acts. Taking the human body as his basic unit of measurement, he saw this space as something like that defined by a gyroscope, whose basic positions consist of six directions and three surfaces: forward and back, left and right, up and down, horizontal, perpendicular, and vertical. The practical applications[3] to dance of this notion of the kinesphere were probably Laban's own original contribution, but for the people of Western Europe the notion of the kinesphere was hardly new. Leonardo da Vinci did a rough sketch, based on a book of architecture [de Architectura c. 27 B.C.] by the ancient Roman, Vitruvius, in which a well-developed human body fit precisely within the

---

[1]This translation is from Iwabuchi Keisuke, "Butō no Paradaimu," Butōki, no. 3 (1982), unpaginated.

[2]Here Iwabuchi uses the term sōzōrittai (imaginary three-dimensional space), to translate into Japanese Laban's term, "kinesphere." The term is defined in Laban's book, Choreutics, as "the sphere around the body whose periphery can be reached by easily extended limbs...We are able to outline the boundary of this imaginary sphere with our feet as well as with our hands." Rudolf Laban, Choreutics (London: MacDonald and Evans, 1966), p. 10.

[3]These applications include Laban's theory of dance notation, called "Labanotation," as well as his ideas on dance education.

diagram created by superimposing a square on a circle. Albrecht Durer, who learned from Leonardo's example, also believed that each part of the body is in symmetrical proportion, and he left us numerous sketches of various ways to draw those proportions. Therefore, Laban's kinesphere might also be described as that idealized space, the microcosm, which since the time of ancient Greece has been seen as enveloping the human being.

The second explanation is the familiar one that the origin of dance is in mimicry. One imitates some object or animal's actions and facial expressions. One starts to feel one has become a bird or animal, running water, a tree which rustles in the breeze. Dance originates in the pleasure we take in copying. Among other things, it is said that philosophy had its origins in this discovery of the possibilities for resemblance. Mimicry and mime, however, developed into public entertainments that invited laughter. When you look at the traditional dances of India and Java, you can see imitations of nature in abundance. In Indian dance, for example, to create the form of a bird with wings flapping, the right and left palms are crossed, the inside of the thumbs are placed together, and the rest of the fingers are fluttered. In the pantomime of Marcel Marceau, the flittering departure of a butterfly is "imitated" by the twisting neck and the expression in the eyes of the man who watches it disappear.

It seems to me, however, that when you divide the origin of dance into these two explanations (the instinct theory based on the limitations of the body and the theory that imitation institutes culture), we lose sight of dance per se and they almost end up being explanations of the ancient origins of athletics and drama. There's something else troubling me: that the Butō style of groups such as Hoppō Butō-ha and Suzuran-tō doesn't seem to fit very well into this standard cultural history of Western style dance.

For example, those forms of dance which are similar to athletics, seeking to develop the health and beauty of the body as a microcosm of the universe, are permeated with a will that aims for the symmetry and unification of the body. Butō, on the other hand, shows us a body in which, from the start, balance has been destroyed, twisted, warped, and crushed. And the will which seeks to unify is also destroyed, as the Butō dancer attempts to release the deeply repressed unconscious.

Dance which mimics or mimes depends on imitations of the object to capture the object as a generalized form. In Nō, when the shite[4] looks down and covers his face with his palm, it appears as though he were restraining

---

[4]The shite is the main character in a Nō drama.

tears; this kata⁵ for crying is called the shiori kata. Recently, at the Cultural Agency's Traveling Arts Festival (November 29, 1980, Otaru City Hall, Hokkaido), there was a performance of Nō and Kyōgen. Even in this performance of Aoi no Ue, Tōkio Otsubo of the Hōsho school, who played the living spirit of Rokujō (the Lady of the 6th Ward), paused at the hashigakari⁶ to say, "There is no human form here, not even a person to whom I may address this question" and then performed the shiori kata.

Unlike these other forms of dance, the Butō dance of Hoppō Butō-ha and Suzuran-tō does not originate in imitation. The body of the Butō dancer convulses endlessly. It as though each fiber of the muscles has its own selfish autonomy and shudders violently as it pleases. It is not some kata that cries or is sad, it is the muscles themselves that are crying. The will does not move the muscles, the muscles themselves have their own will. The trembling of the limbs infects the spectator watching, too; this will of the muscles calls forth the penetrating power of the imagination so that mutual communication between audience and dancer occurs. Rather than communicating stereotyped emotions through patterns of dance that imitate, Butō comes to have a more direct effect on the spectator.

If we compare the terms buyō and butō, "bu" has a meaning that resembles the word shoga (pantomimic dancing). The character "yō" refers to the kind of movement that closely follows the music (ongaku ni noru), whereas "tō" refers to the movement of stamping feet which gives rise to rhythm, to the treading of a regulated step from which one acquires a feeling of pleasure. However, in this essay, both buyō and butō will be used similarly, to mean "dance" in the older, wider sense of the word.⁷ I've taken the position

---

⁵Although the word kata can have a range of meanings, here it basically means a traditional dance pattern.

⁶The Nō stage "bridge" which is used for the main actors' entrances and exits.

⁷What Iwabuchi is referring to here is the fact that the relative meanings of the Japanese words butō and buyō have shifted in the last 10-15 years. It used to be that buyō referred to traditional Japanese dance forms, and butō referred to everything else (e.g. the waltz, the hula, etc.). Nowadays butō is often used to refer specifically to the dance movement influenced by Hijikata's Ankoku Butō, while the meaning of buyō has shifted to include Western-style dance. Iwabuchi along with other dance critics uses the word butō to refer **both** to Western-influenced dance in general **and** dance influenced by Ankoku Butō in particular. In order to differentiate between

that from kagura[8] to German "modern Tanz," buyō and butō share the distinctive characteristic that they are **dance.**

In Laban's kinesphere, the basic stance is that of the human rising up, like a tower. In contrast to that, the basic position in the dance of Hoppō Butō-ha and Suzuran-tō is horizontal, level with, or below the earth's surface. They tumble, bow low, lie down sideways, or sleep facing up. In this way they are able to experience the viewpoint of insects and animals. The act of crouching down, with arms hugging knees to make themselves as small as possible, is a compression of the self's center, perhaps a reversion to the seed, egg, embryo, chrysalis, cocoon. In the pause in which the dancer stands on his tiptoes, he seems suspended by an invisible thread. There are scenes in which the dancers actually disappear, hauled up by copper wires, or are, conversely, lowered onto the stage. This movement upward and downward might be a metaphor for the renunciation and invasion of the earth's surface, which is used as a boundary to make "above" and "below" into mirror images. The rise and fall of bodies could also be seen as an escape to heaven or an infiltration of hell. In a tree, the branches and twigs above are balanced by an equal quantity of roots below. Above and below exist to mirror each other's image of the world. The kinesphere of Hoppō Butō-ha causes the echo of both reality and illusion to resound between the space above and below the horizon line.

There is also the sphere of animism, in which animals and insects live together. In the world of kanji [Japanese ideograms], the character for insect [虫] is the general term for animal. Birds are "flying insects," caterpillars are "hairy insects," turtles are "shelled insects," and the "naked insect" is man. **All** insects share in common a kinesphere made up of the horizontal plane, the space above, and the space below. This way of looking at humans, as naked insects, enables one to understand another expressive form used by Butō dancers, [called beshimi after the grimace mask used in Nō drama]. In this dance movement Butō dancers show the whites of their eyes, twist their mouths, bare their teeth, and spew out their tongues, completely destroying their own faces. Why do they do it? Ordinarily, for us, as members of society, the preservation of our sense of personal identity is considered a duty. Nowadays, the value of individuality is defined as the dignity of being independent and standing up to the huge organization of state and society.

---

the two usages, in **my** translations, I've capitalized butō when I feel the author is referring to the Butō **movement** (e.g., "Butō breaks through all verbal definitions...") and simply used the word "dance" to translate the other usage.

[8]Kagura is an ancient form of Japanese court dance.

However, individuals are in constant competition, always comparing themselves to others. It is an enormous strain to have to continuously maintain one's sense of separate individuality in the face of this kind of contradiction, and the waste of energy involved inevitably leads to suffering. If one neglects for even a moment the effort to maintain one's individuality, the pressure that our "information society" (jōhō shakai)[9] wields to force us into homogeneity will violate the individual, render him powerless, abandon, and eliminate him. Actually, the face of the individual is a symbol: a proof that the individual identity is still being preserved in our society. Therefore, the act of walking the streets in sunglasses becomes a partial renunciation of identity, a concealment, a refuge from the coercion of society. We all know that this kind of escape from the preservation of a sense of individual identity happens often. The Butō beshimi may seem to at first to be simply an expression of deep-rooted hatred, but there is more to it than that; there's a denial in it that relies on the destruction of the equation face=individuality=identity. It also incorporates, among other things, a renunciation of the myth of respect for the individual, as well as a kind of magic that attempts to regenerate both man's sense of being alive, and the power of primitive life, through a return to man as the "naked insect." For example, when you try to imitate the Butō dancers, and you look at your own face, which you have distorted with all your might, you will probably notice that you have acquired a sense of spiritual unity and tranquility, a sensation of having no thoughts, similar to that acquired through Zen meditation. The personality, which has been straining so hard to stay separate, fuses and is reborn in the "man" who is a "thing." The Butō dancer's voiceless laughter is another example of a frequently performed kata that provides this kind of release and salvation.

The enjoyable duty thus falls to us, the audience in which the power of the imagination has been stimulated, to try to assign the dance of Hoppō Butō-ha and Suzuran-tō to a position within the cultural history of modern dance (in the broad sense of the term), and to attempt to extract from the dance we've seen the fundamental principles, that is, the paradigm, of Butō.

---

[9]The phrase jōhō shakai is usually taken to refer to both the control of the masses through the image-centered information conveyed by the media and the bureaucratic over-management of capitalist consumer societies.

Appendix C

"On Ankoku Butō"

by

Gōda Nario

On May 24, 1959, at the 6th Annual Newcomer's Performance held in Tokyo by the All-Japan Art Dance Association (now called the Modern Dance Association[1]), Hijikata Tatsumi's dance piece, <u>Kinjiki</u> (Forbidden Colors), was performed.[2] If this performance had not taken place, today's modern dance world would be an entirely different place. As a matter of fact, no matter what criteria for inclusion you might use for a history of modern dance in Japan since 1959, it would be inconceivable to leave out Ankoku Butō, which was founded by Hijikata Tatsumi and was the crux of all the Butō movement's subsequent expansion and development.

Of course, from a broader perspective, Ankoku Butō actually takes up only one small corner of the area that the Butō movement occupies in today's dance world. However, because of all the dance movements developed in this quarter century, Ankoku Butō was filled with the greatest intellectual rigor, dances influenced by it have been the deepest philosophically and have had the widest impact. The vital energy of this truly brilliant era in dance has been generated by the Butō movement, by Ankoku Butō, and above all, by Hijikata Tatsumi. To put it another way, during this period, Hijikata's superlative sensitivity developed each dancer's individuality and through their dance performance revealed existence, that is, the body's true state, which lies in dance. By this means dance was transformed and deepened until it reached the level of a personal philosophy of life or an epistemology. An achievement

---

[1]In Japanese, the <u>Zen-Nihon Geijutsu Buyō Kyōkai</u>, which is now called the <u>Gendai Buyō Kyōkai</u>.

[2]This translation is from Gōda Nario, "Ankoku Butō ni Tsuite," in <u>Butō: Nikutai no Suriarisutotachi</u> (Butō: Surrealists of the Flesh), ed. Hanaga Mitsutoshi (Tokyo: Gendai Shokan, 1983), unpaginated.

79

of this kind was not to be found in our dance history up till then, and it was an innovative influence not only on dance but on the closely related arts, especially theater. I hear that in the West, Ankoku Butō and the Butō movement, which are Hijikata's creations, are now causing a big splash. Forbidden Colors was the first stone that Hijikata threw.

At the time it was difficult to say whether the ripples from that stone were big or small, because Hijikata was almost immediately hounded out of the contemporary dance world and his influence was completely, one might even say politically, crushed. However, he had already acquired the support of Mishima Yukio (upon whose novel he had based his dance); in addition, his existence was getting wider attention from those working outside dance. In any case, the greatest significance of Forbidden Colors lay in its demonstration of the way in which the substance of Mishima's novel could be clearly conveyed through a dance. The dance was performed by two males, a man and a boy; a white chicken was strangled to death over the boy's crotch and then in the darkness there were footsteps, the sounds of the boy escaping and the man pursuing him. This performance thrust before the dance world the fact that here was a work that rendered unnecessary the systems and methods ordinarily relied upon by mainstream dance. It is my opinion that Forbidden Colors was probably the first truly innovative dance piece done in Japan since the inception of Western-style modern dance in the early Taisho era, because it discarded the music upon which dance leans, the mediation of interpretive program notes, even the technique in which the dancers believed.

Another decisive point [in our evaluation of the place of Forbidden Colors in the history of dance] would be that the fusion of dance with the darkness of existence, which formed the basis for the structure of Forbidden Colors, has characterized Ankoku Butō ever since. After it, Ankoku Butō, especially in the 70's, developed various techniques. Its realm of expression expanded to the point where it even included crisply dry, emotionless work--quite at odds with the style of irrationality and horror with which Butō is usually associated. There was never any compromise with reality, however: the darkness of existence itself continued to be protected. Even if by borrowing the forms of things just as they were, Butō was able to approach our everyday sense of pleasure in elegance or quiet contemplation, before we knew it, we were enticed to the point where there was too much elegance, too much contemplation; and Butō had exposed the ruin which dwells in elegance, the death which stains contemplation. In this way the expressive techniques used were kept firmly in line with the goal of portraying the darkness of our existence.

At the same time, however, although darkness blanketed the stage, this did not mean that Hijikata forgot to be concerned with the expression of such things as a feeling of faint hope or a glimmer of gentle detachment. Did I write "concern"? It was not concern exactly--it should rather be understood as the result of an delicate balance between the confidence Hijikata placed in his own splendid reach as a superb creative artist, and his inner will power; in other words, his inner will power and his actual performance.

Although Forbidden Colors only lasted a few minutes, it combined the barbarous act of strangling a chicken with the treatment of the anti-social and supposedly taboo topic of homosexuality. It made those of us who watched it to the end shudder, but once the shudder passed through our bodies, it resulted in a refreshing sense of release. Perhaps there was a darkness concealed within our bodies similar to that found in Forbidden Colors and which therefore responded to it with a feeling of liberation. Hijikata's debut work Forbidden Colors actually expanded the range of dance; through it he forced us to experience not only the excellence of his style but also the abyss of existence, and by this means developed a theory of the body for all future dance.

We had the good fortune, in April 1983, to be able to spend eight days experiencing Hijikata's recent work, Keshiki ni Itton no Kamigata (Towards Scenery--A One Ton Hairdo). Hijikata's comeback, along with Ashikawa Yōko, was a hot topic of conversation. Hijikata had not danced in any new works since November 1968, and Ashikawa had not performed in public for seven years. Speculations were rife about what kind of transformations we would see. I myself discerned a number of changes in Hijikata's work: to begin with, this piece was very lengthy and was divided up into three parts: "Supein ni Sakura" (Cherry Trees in Spain), "Plan-B Ji Mosha" (The Duplicate Temple of Plan B) and "Hijō ni Kyūsoku na Kyūkisei Bromaido" (Bromide That Can Be Inhaled Incredibly Quickly).[3] Secondly, whereas the excellence of Hijikata's previous pieces had consisted in their quality of painstaking care, comparable to what you might use in digging a mine shaft, the excellence of the new work consisted in the way that the space, in which bits and pieces were left scattered like objects set completely adrift, was transformed at a single stroke into a gorgeous mandala. In some sense it was as though a closed world had been transformed into an open one--now there was an extravagant freedom and a startlingly intense power of representation.

---

[3] The English translations of the above titles are really quite speculative--this was the best that could be done without more information on the performances. "Plan B" is an avant-garde theater in Tokyo.

There was only one main theme to be drawn out of the work as a whole, however: namely, how pathetically wretched it was that an old woman's last sexual act should be an act of masturbation dependent on fantasy. It was this misery that, making visceral the unending darkness of sexuality, resulted in a moment of stifling impact. Up till that moment, we had assumed that what we saw in the first and second sections of the work was "real." In the third section, however, those fragments from the previous dances that had been floating disordered within us, suddenly fell into place and we realized that they were all figments of the old woman's imagination. Every one of the fantasies was about hairpieces that weighed a ton. In the last section, an epilogue was attached in which the old woman departed burdened down with several of the wigs. A sense of human life clearly lingered on in the them, expressing the unchangeable difficulties of old age. What Hijikata wanted to convey by this means, however, was something about **everyone's** experience of life: how it is that in an instant, the instant we call "now," the reality of our entire existence could became a dream. It was an attempt to extract the sexuality which lies at the deepest core of existence; the grotesque sexuality that we cannot deny.

Towards Scenery--One Ton of Wigs leapt 24 years into the past to share a point in common with Forbidden Colors: the character of the old woman can be seen as a logical extension of the character of the young boy. Incidently, a little less than a year before Forbidden Colors, Hijikata had had an idea for his debut piece, but it was rejected. The concept was that on stage a chicken should be killed by hanging it upside-down by the neck. This was the concept realized in the 1968 piece Nikutai no Hanran (Revolt of the Flesh). In the dance motif of "killing a chicken," which Forbidden Colors and Revolt of the Flesh share, one could plainly see the turbulent passion of the boy's youthful flesh, an expression of a dark sexuality which he could neither control nor be set free from. However, between the impression we got from seeing this, and what the boy himself probably felt, there seemed to be a rather large gap. This gap in meaning was made possible by the range of sensibilities that were liberated in us by Forbidden Colors.[4]

In a sense, the whole of Forbidden Colors is based on something exceedingly natural; its acts of brutality too are in accord with the realities of

---

[4]Another possible interpretation of this sentence might be: "This gap in meaning was made possible by the differing emotional responses that Forbidden Colors released in the audience when it came into contact with their wide range of sensibilities."

nature. Actually, in the farming village in Akita where Hijikata spent his boyhood, people lived in familiar proximity with horses and chickens. Because of this, strangling a chicken meant there would be a treat; it was a rare event surrounded with the excitement of a special hospitality or festival. The progression from strangling the chicken, to cooking it, to presenting it on the dinner table was apparent even to a child. Although the boy in Forbidden Colors directed the release of his dark passion, which burst forth from the inner depths of his flesh, towards the chicken, this passion might be regarded as a form of love, as part of a natural cycle that occurred occasionally in everyday farming life. Looking at it from this perspective, wasn't the homosexuality taken from Mishima's book, which so surprised the audience, simply the visual form given to this natural kind of love? In any event, I am now thoroughly convinced of this point at least: Hijikata did not budge an inch from his commitment to the close examination of the relationship between existence and sexuality, a relationship whose manifestations come bursting forth from the abyss of darkness.

Already much has been said about Hijikata Tatsumi and Ankoku Butō. There are a number of essays about their shifting trends: for example, about their early preference for the works of such iconoclastic European literary figures as Genet, Lautréamont, and the Marquis de Sade; or about the 1972 performance Tōhoku Kabuki (Northern Kabuki) which signalled [in its revival of interest in indigenous Japanese theatrical forms] a kind of "return to Japan" (Nihon kaiki). These essays have come to play an important supporting role in the evolution of Ankoku Butō. However, while full of valuable insights, none of them have approached the source of Hijikata's creativity, or the structure of Ankoku Butō which corresponds to it. In fact, a proper essay has yet to be written; an essay which would, for example, critically acclaim Ankoku Butō as the avant garde within the Butō movement, and evaluate the historical grounds that brought it forth. Such an essay would paint the **whole** picture, showing Ankoku Butō towering over the rest of the modern dance world; furthermore, it would be about how Ankoku Butō has secured a special preserve unto itself, luminous and brilliant, within the world history of dance in this century. One of these days, these questions will be elucidated authoritatively, but for now...

Well, to return to the common thread that I mentioned before, which runs between Forbidden Colors and Towards Scenery--A Ton of Wigs--I wonder where it came from? Recently Hijikata's autobiographical work, Yameru Mai Hime (A Dancer's Sickness), was published (March 1983). In every one of its chapters, the stage was set with scenery from his youth. He describes the golden light of his home's northern side and back garden; the incessant shower of cicadas whose poignant sound impressed itself into his chest like a tattoo; the moment by moment change in the light as the sun went down, and how as he looked into the sun an image of his sister appeared like a shadow in the instant just before it set, and he was swept up in the twilight's enchantment; and how the young man, quick to hear from whence the wind came and whither it went, perceived, long ago, the inner life of his own body.

He could not help letting those he loved--his mother and father, older sisters--dwell within his body. Even a boy who could cheerfully endure nature's violence, could not understand the economic depression of the times in farming villages like Akita. Nevertheless, hadn't he scented more accurately than we that the darkness of the shadows cast by those farming people who stood in nature's light, was the darkness of existence? He understood this because he kept within himself the misery of his sister's departure for a far distant place.[5]

Around the middle of the 1960's, when he was first advocating Ankoku Butō, Hijikata started to grow his hair out, probably to help keep alive the sister who dwelt within him. In the 70's, it was the old prostitute who followed a life of suffering that appeared as a symbol in Hijikata's Butō. Hijikata didn't take one false step away from Ankoku Butō: his work achieved a scale of exquisite gentleness, calm, and even magnanimity enriched by Hijikata's continuous inner dialogue with both his sister and his own youth.

In October of 1968 Hijikata held a solo dance performance at the former Japanese Youth Hall (Nihon Seinen-kan). The name of the piece was Nihonjin to Hijikata Tatsumi (The Japanese and Hijikata Tatsumi), but it is better known as Nikutai no Hanran (Revolt of the Flesh). Considering Hijikata's career after that performance, one might say that it was a turning point; or that it should be understood as signalling a "return to Japan" (Nihon kaiki); or you might say that, as you'd expect from its subtitle, people just went wild over the body's revolt. None of the above alternatives would be entirely mistaken, I feel. However, it appears to me now that those of us who, with smug complacency, pointed this dance out as a turning point, or were ecstatic with enthusiasm, were actually being sharply rebuked from the stage. I believe this because I cannot forget the confusion into which this one

---

[5]What the author seems to mean here is that although the farming people lived in close proximity with the beauty of nature, they had to live with its harshness as well. One of the results of the harsh economic reality of farming life in Japan was the common practice of selling daughters into prostitution; the implication of the last sentence seems to be that Hijikata's eldest sister fell victim to this traditional way of supporting the family.

spectator was plunged at simultaneously feeling that I was being held in contempt--I do not know any dancer who is as arrogant as Hijikata is on the stage--yet at the same time feeling absolutely compelled to watch his every move.

It is because of precisely this feeling of ambivalence that I have returned to Hijikata and his art over and over again. Strange to say, now I have the feeling I understand why it is that he rejected everything--the audience, the dancers, established dance, Western iconoclastic writers--and attempted, on that stage, to vanish into the shadowy void. It was because Hijikata was determined that there be no relation between the environment in which his body--a body in which the boy lived, the sister dwelt--had to go on living and the site where culture, art, and dance are enjoyed. What was called the Butō of Hijikata was simply his body, inhabited by his sister, walking about, and those Butō dancers who couldn't understand this departed one by one. It was having been left all alone that provoked him to plunge headlong into the desperate frenzy of <u>Revolt of the Flesh</u>.

In 1970, Hijikata presented under his direction a group of unknown dancers, among them Ashikawa Yōko,[6] signalling the group's formation by hanging out a sign board inscribed with the words, "Hangi Daitō-kan" (A Model for a Grand Dance of Burnt Sacrifice[7]). The sign was a splendid piece of calligraphy by Mishima Yukio. Hangi Daitō-kan took the great dance of nature as its model, burning, sacrificing the body for others. In sum, this dance principle expressed the idea that only by throwing off the body and transcending suffering can true dance be created, and that Butō **begins** with the abandonment of self. This was Hijikata's sincere resolve at the time, and it has become the position of later Ankoku Butō as well. The stress on the corporeal existence of the body in Butō began with <u>Revolt of the Flesh</u>.

How did this concept of bodily existence make its appearance, and how did it take shape? The notion of the sister living within his body was for Hijikata a concrete starting point. Through Hijikata's skillful questioning of his own body, he revealed to us its birth and formation; that is, he returned to the landscape of Akita. Then, he set Ashikawa and the other dancers the difficult task of becoming animals such as horses or cats. What Hijikata probably had in mind was an attempt to restore the body to its natural state

---

[6]Ashikawa Yōko is a dancer known particularly for her work with Hijikata. Although she has not performed in the U.S., she and Tanaka Min toured Europe in 1983 performing Hijikata's choreography.

[7]Again, this translation is speculative.

by infusing it with the principle that for anything to become its own locus of expression[8] it must first fit into the grand scheme of nature. By having the dancers become animals he was trying to let them see what it would be like to leave behind their own bodies, and at the same time leave behind their easy assumption that the body can become an expressive tool simply through its everyday experience or through mainstream dance training.

Rather than a weak body, governed by reason and emotion, and satisfied with those, Hijikata wanted a body that was powerful, gentle, and flexible, in which reason was manifested and emotions were generated as the **result** of physical action. In a sense he believed that all Butō must be created from the body. Even in Forbidden Colors, which I mentioned at the beginning of this essay, Hijikata was carrying out these ideas unconsciously, and it is natural to infer from this that even then Hijikata was restricting the body's expressiveness to the parameters of its structure and what it could realistically perform. To put it plainly, instead of loading up the body with imaginative elements and then having this so-called "body" take flight, he invited space and time **into** the body, and by means of the littlest possible bodily expression, extracted an enormous amount. In mainstream dance, pieces and scenes are constructed from the outside, solely on the basis of a body that expresses itself externally, whereas Butō attempts to affirm the dance which lives **within** the body--the body is, in itself, contemplated as a small universe--and its structure and performance are thus revitalized. Taking the body as his premise, Hijikata boldly restricted his work to the body's concrete structure. Then he went even further, placing strict limits on time and space too, at least as they affect the dance. Normally, space and time impress us as having a certain continuity. We enjoy a pleasant feeling of intoxicating freedom from the continuously flowing movement of dance, or the moment by moment change in the scene before us. Dance that plays on this impression by the audience has a tendency to race off in a freely visionary direction. This then has the surprising effect of dragging dance down to an everyday level, confining it to an unexpectedly cramped space. In Revolt of the Flesh, Hijikata rejected our common sense notions of continuity, slicing through time and space. Western dances that are quite sensible, such as the polka or the waltz, appeared before us distorted and chopped up, in order to overturn our preconceived ideas.

This was not the only reason that Hijikata added restrictions on time and space, however; he was probably also trying to turn to his own advantage the fact that the body is a bundle of sensations, an accumulation of sensory experiences of finite time and space. Making the body an incarnation of time

---

[8]Or: acquire its own subjective voice.

and space, Hijikata tried to fill it with **real** time and space. He did this by fragmenting motion into articulated movements that expressed precisely the temporary forms of each moment, and then entrusting the dance to the accumulation of those momentary changes in time and space.

Generally, Butō has come to be thought of as something ambiguous, grotesque. However, in Butō the environment that affects the body is very natural. Butō attempts to return the abstract, generalized body to its original place, which might be an unknown flower that blooms in the meadow, a lofty tree, a cricket that cries beneath the earth, a horse that gallops through the fields. The loveliness, gentleness, fierceness, and beauty of all these comes from nothing other than their ability to artlessly adapt themselves to natural laws.

As I mentioned before, only in Hijikata's Butō was there a deep connection between the body itself and the sister who dwelt within. The life of that sister was the motive which drove Hijikata to dance; it was the key to his creation of Ankoku Butō. Accordingly, Hijikata had to concretely fulfill the promise made to his sister. Luckily, we were able to ascertain that relatively early in his career, in the dance movement of Hangi Daitō-kan, he had fulfilled that promise.

In September of 1972, about a month after the Butō group Harupin's performance of <u>Nagasu Kujira</u> (Razorback Whale), Hijikata and Ankoku Butō's epoch-making Art Theater performance of <u>Shiki no Tame no 27 Ban</u> (27 Nights for 4 Seasons) was held. Their technique in this performance was simple, but this performance not only decisively established the style of Ankoku Butō in the 1970's, it contained the innovation that raised Butō to the status of an international dance movement: that is, walking bowlegged (<u>ganimata</u>). In <u>ganimata</u> the weight is hung on the outer sides of the two legs. When one "floats" the inside of the legs upwards, the knees will turn out of their own accord, and the entire frame of the body sinks down. The important point here is that this technique contrasts sharply with the ballet technique of standing on pointe, in which the body is made to float upwards and appears transformed into an otherworldly being. However, I don't mean to say that this is a contrast in the sense that walking bowlegged makes the body more **realistic**--having the frame of the body sink is just as unrealistic a technique as standing on the toes. If standing on pointe in ballet creates an imaginary space floating 15 centimeters above the stage, the bowlegged stance creates one hovering 15 centimeters below. But again, this was not the **only** reason that Ankoku Butō came into being and became a major international dance form.

It was Hijikata's superb sensitivity that quickly and skillfully drew together his own deep personal experiences involving his sister, establishing a core from which the various techniques of Butō bloomed. This core, which was essentially his sister, was already understood to be in his body when he made his proclamation to Ankoku Butō in 1968. It reached full maturity with Ashikawa's dual portrayal of an old woman, standing rigidly, and of a Moon Maiden who made her body as fully round as a drop of water on the grass. In an instant, the old woman saw her past drifting just where fate would have it go, while an endless dream of eternity seemed to dwell in the smile of the Moon Maiden. Feelings of detachment and hope were born and emerged like trees from the earth, towering above the innocent maiden and the Night Cherry Maiden of Confusion (Sakuran no Yosakura Hime) who blossomed, accompanied by a droll-faced carp and a childishly pompous devil. The space that in this way came into being was charged full of time and, indeed, was elevated to the level of a philosophy of life and an epistemology. This was how Ankoku Butō finally came to crystalize into the dance form that we know today, one of the truly great dance innovations of this century.

I'd like to say in conclusion, that in compliance with my friend Hanaga's wishes, I had planned on dealing with all of Butō, but having stumbled into the subject of Ankoku Butō, I got sidetracked and failed to accomplish what I had set out to do. I really should apologize for the fact that I failed to mention the dancer Ohno Kazuo, whose Gekiyaku no Buyōka (Dancer of Drastic Measures) Hijikata admired for its lofty individuality. I regret this very much, and I only hope that I might be granted another opportunity to write on this subject.

"My View of Hoppō Butō-ha"

by

Eguchi Osamu

"All phenomena, in their discordant state, are inserted into the mind, which is like a register that records and exchanges them for cultural values; like a black box...." I was trapped by this kind of thinking, oppressed by a sense that there was no way out, when I encountered Hoppō Butō-ha.[1]

The fingertips remained relaxed, although inside they were filled with tension; in the movements of a body attempting to take the form of all things, there was a delicate rhythm that resembled the ebb and flow of the tide; there were stances taken, spaces to pause in which discordances were skillfully brought together; finally, there was a vision of a poisonous devil whose love concealed the darkness within.... What I saw on that stage was a world in which words and things had not yet been differentiated; in short, I beheld the dawn of the world.

Butō breaks through all verbal definitions and snatches away the audience's sensibilities to a state of nakedness. Watching it, I suddenly remembered the words of Paul Valéry: "Dance is certainly a systematized form of action; however [these actions are not motivated by some goal outside of themselves], it is **within** movement itself that dance attains its perfection. Dance is not **going** anywhere. Even if it were pursuing something, that goal would be no more than one state, one pleasure; or perhaps the extreme of ecstacy, of life, the peak of existence--it is merely these things that it seeks and nothing more."[2]

Butō is like poetry in that it, in its very essence, resists the substitutive function in which words are used to express some **thing**. In poetry it is the

---

[1]This translation is from Eguchi Osamu, "Hoppo Butō-ha 'Shiken,'" Butōki, no. 2 (1980), p. 9.

[2]Translated from the Japanese.

words, in Butō it is the body--the body's movement encloses within **itself** the extreme point which it must seek, while, at the same time, by twisting, jostling, and touching it opens up a unique symbolic space to enfold both the reader and the spectator. Needless to say, within that symbolic space, any explanation which takes the form, "this means so-and-so," becomes meaningless. The order of values which the register has built up so assiduously, turns to nonsense in a moment. It becomes instead a mandala woven from words and resemblances which, as it whirls around, creates correspondences between all things. Even in a world where the loss of the sacred has long since been recognized, to destroy the hierarchical order of values might be seen as the work of the devil. Or again, we might compare the practitioner of Butō to a priest who has mastered the Sabbath rituals that invite generation after generation into a thickly entangled world, a world of darkness that our modern age has lost, where the gap between words and things disappears and where existence unfolds before us.

Despite these thoughts, the nightmare of the mind as a register still continues to haunt my steps, refusing to leave me alone. The empire of verbal language, whose **essence** lies in the function of articulation [that is, the separation of words and things], is extremely powerful. As Roland Barthes has said, "language is essentially violence: we have been besieged for generation after generation by the network of meaning that the metaphoric function extends around us, so that to the people it encloses this network has come to seem as if it is itself the world."[3] It is in this way that human beings are domesticated. This network of meaning is, precisely, our black box. Once one gets used to using it, one may not even be aware of it at all. Moreover, this metaphoric function isn't just one person's exclusive property. Apparently it is distributed quite evenly. Is there any more perfect way to control people than that?

Now, what is it that has made this network possible? It's the detachment of words from things. Language, which comes into existence through a union of mutually interacting elements, depends on the fact that words are separated from things to be able to function more quickly and freely. Then, the network of meaning, which is based on the metaphoric function, establishes itself as a kind of pseudo-nature--in a sense, it could be said that it is this network which rears the human being.

Speaking pessimistically, I wonder if man hasn't completely lost the ability to directly confront things-in-themselves. If accidentally encountered,

---

[3]Unable to locate the original; translated from the Japanese.

perhaps things-in-themselves would completely smash humans.... However, perhaps I have become **too** pessimistic. Even if the destruction of the black box is impossible, don't we have the stage of Hoppō Butō-ha, which has the power to create a twist in the network of meaning?

The body of the Butō dancer regresses to the depths of existence, and by means of cyclical movement reaches the heights. I will, for a time, be guided by their inviting hands, and swim into the depths full of the pungent smell of existence.

Bibliography of Works Cited

Books

Bachelard, Gaston. The Poetics of Space. Boston: Beacon Press, 1969.

Berger, Peter and Thomas Luckmann. The Social Construction of Reality. New York: Anchor Books, 1967.

Bethe, Monica and Karen Brazell. "Dance in the Nō Theater." Cornell East Asia Papers, no. 29. Ithaca, NY: China-Japan Program, 1982.

Blacker, Carmen. The Catalpa Bow. London: George Allen and Unwin, 1986.

Dowsey, Stuart J., ed. Zengakuren: Japan's Revolutionary Students (Berkeley, CA: The Ishi Press, 1970).

Freud, Sigmund. "The 'Uncanny.'" In Studies in Parapsychology. Translated by Alix Strachey. Edited by Philip Rieff. New York: Collier Books, 1977.

Haga, Tōru. "The Japanese Point of View." In Avant-Garde Art in Japan. New York: Harry N. Abrams, Inc., 1962.

Hanaga, Mitsutoshi, ed. Butō: Nikutai no Suriarisutotachi (Butō: Surrealists of the Flesh). Tokyo: Gendai Shokan, 1983.

Hane, Mikiso. Peasants, Rebels, and Outcastes. New York: Pantheon Books, 1982.

Harpham, Geoffrey Galt. On the Grotesque: Strategies of Contradiction in Art and Literature. Princeton, NJ: Princeton University Press, 1982.

Havens, Thomas R. H. Artist and Patron in Postwar Japan. Princeton: Princeton University Press, 1982.

Hijikata, Tatsumi. Yameru Mai Hime (A Dancer's Sickness). Tokyo: Hakusuisha, 1983.

Komparu, Kunio. The Noh Theater: Principles and Perspectives. Translated by Jane Corddry and Steven Comee. New York, Weatherhill, 1983.

Koschmann, J. Victor, ed. Authority and the Individual in Japan. Tokyo: University of Tokyo Press, 1978.

Koschmann, J. Victor, Ōiwa Keibō and Yamashita Shinji, eds. "International Perspectives on Yanagita Kunio and Folklore Studies." Cornell East Asia Papers, no. 37. Ithaca, NY: China-Japan Program, 1985.

Kuniyoshi, Kazuko. "An Overview of the Contemporary Dance Scene." Orientation Seminars on Japan, no. 19. Tokyo: Japan Foundation, 1985.

Laban, Rudolf. Choreutics. London: MacDonald and Evans, 1966.

Packard, George R. Protest in Tokyo: The Security Treaty Crisis of 1960. Princeton: Princeton University Press, 1966.

Seidensticker, Edward. Low City, High City. New York: Alfred A. Knopf, 1983.

Tanizaki, Jun'ichirō. In Praise of Shadows. Translated by Thomas J. Harper and Edward Seidensticker. New Haven, CT: Leete's Island Books, Inc., 1977.

Wigman, Mary. The Language of Dance. Translated by Walter Sorell. Middletown, CT: Wesleyan University Press, 1966.

Yamaguchi, Masao. "Kingship, Theatricality, and Marginal Reality in Japan." In Text and Context: The Social Anthropology of Tradition. Edited by Ravindra K. Jain. Philadelphia: Institute for the Study of Human Issues, 1977.

Journal and Newspaper Articles

Barba, Eugenio. "Theater Anthropology." The Drama Review 26 (Summer 1982), pp. 5-33.

Croce, Arlene. "Dancing in the Dark." New Yorker 60 (19 November 1985), p. 171.

David, Martin A. "Sankai Juku." High Performance 7, no. 3 (1985), p. 18.

Dunning, Jennifer. "Birth of Butō Recalled by Founder." New York Times, 20 November 1985, p. C27.

--------. "Sankai Juku at City Center." New York Times, 2 November 1984.

Eguchi, Osamu. "Hoppō Butō-ha 'Shiken'" (My View of Hoppō Butō-ha). Butōki, no. 2 (1980), p. 9.

Goodman, David. "New Japanese Theater." The Drama Review 15 (Spring 1971), pp. 154-168.

Hirosue, Tamotsu. "The Secret Ritual of the Place of Evil." Concerned Theatre Japan 2, no. 1 (1971), pp. 14-21.

Iwabuchi, Keisuke. "Butō no Paradaimu." (The Paradigm of Butō). Butōki, no. 3 (1982), unpaginated.

Jameson, Frederic. "Postmodernism, or The Cultural Logic of Capitalism." New Left Review, no. 146 (July-August 1984).

Kiselgoff, Anna. "The Dance: Montreal Dance Festival." New York Times, 23 September 1985, p. C27.

Koschmann, J. Victor. "The Debate on Subjectivity in Postwar Japan: Foundations of Modernism as a Political Critique." Pacific Affairs 54, no. 4 (Winter 1981-82), pp. 609-631.

Kuniyoshi, Kazuko. "Butoh Chronology: 1959-1984." The Drama Review 30 (Summer 1986), pp. 127-141.

Myerscough, Marie. "Butō Special." Tokyo Journal 4 (February 1985), p. 8-9.

Ohno, Kazuo. "Four Pieces." Translated by Maehata Noriko. Stone Lion Review, no. 9 (Spring 1982), pp. 45-48.

---------. "Selections from the Prose of Kazuo Ohno." Translated by Maehata Noriko. The Drama Review 30 (Summer 1986), pp. 156-162.

---------. "Kazuo Ohno Doesn't Commute." Interview with Richard Schechner. The Drama Review 30 (Summer 1986), pp. 163-169.

Oyama, Shigeō. "Amagatsu Ushio: Avant-garde Choreographer." Japan Quarterly 32 (January-March 1985), pp. 69-72.

Pronko, Leonard. "Kabuki Today and Tomorrow." Comparative Drama 7 (Summer 1972), pp. 103-114.

Richie, Donald. "Japan's Avant-garde Theater." The Japan Foundation Newsletter 7 (April-May 1979), pp. 1-4.

96

Siegel, Marcia. "Flickering Stones." Village Voice, 15 October 1985, pp. 101, 103.

Slater, Lizzie. "The Dead Begin to Run: Kazuo Ohno and Butoh Dance." Dance Theatre Journal, London (Winter 1986), pp. 6-10.

"A Taste of Japanese Dance in Durham." New York Times, Sunday, 4 July 1982, Arts and Leisure section.

Tanaka, Min. "Farmer/Dancer or Dancer/Farmer." Interview with Bonnie Sue Stein. The Drama Review 30 (Summer 1986), pp. 142-151.

---------. "from 'I am an Avant-Garde who Crawls the Earth: Homage to Tatsumi Hijikata.'" Translated by Kobata Kazue. The Drama Review 30 (Summer 1986), pp. 153-155.

Tsuno, Kaitarō. "Poor European Theater." Translated by David Goodman. Concerned Theatre Japan 2, no. 3-4 (Spring 1973), pp. 10-25.

---------. "The Tradition of Modern Theatre in Japan." Translated by David Goodman. Canadian Theater Review 20 (Fall 1978), pp. 8-19.

---------. "The Trinity of Modern Theatre." Translated by David Goodman. Concerned Theatre Japan 1 (Summer 1970), pp. 82-89.

Wilk, David. "Profound Perplexing Sankai Juku." The Christian Science Monitor, 8 November 1984.

Yamamoto, Kiyokazu. "Kara's Vision: The World as Public Toilet." Canadian Theatre Review 20 (Fall 1978), pp. 28-33.

Unpublished Materials

Goodman, David. "Satoh Makoto and the Post-Shingeki Movement in Japanese Contemporary Theatre." Ph.D. diss., Cornell University, 1982.

Nakajima, Natsu. Conversation with author, Tokyo, Japan, 5 February 1988.

Ohno, Kazuo. Interview with author, Ithaca, New York, 25 November 1985.

--------. Interview with author, Boston, Massachusetts, 1 July 1986. Audiotape.

--------. "The Origins of Ankoku Butō." Lecture delivered at Cornell University, 25 November 1985. Audiotape.

Ojima, Ichirō. Interview with author, Otaru, Japan, 10 July 1985.

Yamaguchi, Masao. "Theatrical Space in Japan, a Semiotic Approach." Unpublished manuscript.

Yoshida Teiko and Miura Masashi, conversation with the author, 22 January 1986.

CORNELL EAST ASIA SERIES

FORTHCOMING

Order online: www.einaudi.cornell.edu/eastasia/CEASbooks, or contact Cornell East Asia Series Distribution Center, 369 Pine Tree Rd., Ithaca, NY 14853-2820, USA; toll-free: 1-877-865-2432, fax 607-255-7534, ceas@cornell.edu